DEATH BLOSSOMS

MUMIA

ABU-JAMAL

DEATH BLOSSOMS

REFLECTIONS
FROM A PRISONER
OF CONSCIENCE

FOREWORD BY
CORNEL WEST

PREFACE BY
JULIA WRIGHT

PLOUGH PUBLISHING HOUSE

©1997 The Plough Publishing House
of The Bruderhof Foundation

Farmington PA 15437 USA
Robertsbridge E. Sussex TN32 5DR UK

First Printing	Dec. 1996
Second Printing	Feb. 1997
Third Printing	April 1997
Fourth Printing	Nov. 1998

Cover photo by Charles R. Smith, Jr.
Back cover photo by Thomas Filmyer/WCB
Frontispiece by Jennifer Beach

Library of Congress Cataloging-in-Publication Data

Abu-Jamal, Mumia
    Death Blossoms: reflections from a prisoner of conscience / Mumia Abu-Jamal:
foreword by Cornel West: preface by Julia Wright.
            p.   cm.
    ISBN: 0-87486-086-5
    1. Abu-Jamal, Mumia.   2. Death row inmates – United States –Biography.
3. Afro-American prisoners – United States – Biography.
4. Prisoners' writings. American.   I. Title.
HV8699.U5A33   1997
364.66'092 – dc21
[b]   96-49924
                                                         CIP

Printed in USA

CONTENTS

xi   Foreword

xiii   Preface

xxvii   To the Reader

1   A Write-up for Writing

4   Books and the State

6   Capital Punishment

8   Remembering Moser

11   Politics

12   The Search

24   Thoughts on the Divine

28   Night of Power

32   Material Life

34   Life's Religion

39   Isn't It Odd?

40   Spirit War

43   Imprisonment

44   Christian? Christ-like?

53   Miracles

55   The Faith of Slaves

61   Hope

62   Salt of the Earth

65   Community

69 Men of the Cloth

73 Hate's Unkind Counsel

76 Human Beings

77 The Spider

81 The Fall

82 Children

84 The Creator

85 Father Hunger

89 Mother-loss

91 Meeting with a Killer

94 Dialogue

95 Objectivity and the Media

100 Violence

101 God-talk on Phase II

107 Meditations on the Cross

110 Holiday Thoughts

111 The Wisdom of John Africa

114 Untitled (poem)

115 More War for the Poor

118 Of Becoming

121 A Call to Action

123 Interview with Mumia

151 About the Author

154 Information

TO THOSE

nameless ones who came before

    and are no more,

to those who leapt

    to dark, salty depths,

to those who battled

    against all odds,

to those who would give birth

    to gods,

to those who would not yield –

To those who came before,

to those who are to come,

    I dedicate this shield.

M.A.J.

FOREWORD

Cornel West

The passionate and prophetic voice of Mumia Abu-Jamal challenges us to wrestle with the most distinctive feature of present-day America: the relative erosion of the systems of caring and nurturing. This frightening reality, which renders more and more people unloved and unwanted, results primarily from several fundamental processes. There are, for example, the forces of our unregulated capitalist market, which have yielded not only immoral levels of wealth inequality and economic insecurity but also personal isolation and psychic disorientation. Then there is the legacy of white supremacy, which – in subtle and not-so-subtle ways – continues to produce new forms of geographical segregation, job ceilings, and social tension. We can also see how, in other arenas, oppressive ideologies and persisting bigotries (like patriarchy and homophobia) smother the possibility of healthy and humane relations among men and women. In short, our capitalist "civilization" is killing our minds, bodies, and souls in the name of the American Dream.

As one who has lived on the night-side of this dream –
unjustly imprisoned for a crime he did not commit –
Mumia Abu-Jamal speaks to us of the institutional
injustice and spiritual impoverishment that permeates
our culture. He reminds us of things most fellow citizens would rather deny, ignore, or evade. And, like the
most powerful critics of our society – from Herman
Melville, Theodore Dreiser, and Nathaniel West, to
Ann Petry, Richard Wright, Toni Morrison, and Eugene
O'Neill – he forces us to grapple with the most fundamental question facing this country: what does it profit
a nation to conquer the whole world and lose its soul?

After over fifteen years of nightmarish jail conditions,
Mumia Abu-Jamal's soul is not only intact but still
flourishing – just as the nation's soul withers. Will we
ever listen to and learn from our bloodstained prophets?

Cambridge, Mass.
October 1996

PREFACE

Julia Wright

> Under a government that imprisons any man unjustly,
> the true place for a just man is also a prison.
>
> *Henry David Thoreau, 1817–1862*

> Does the silk-worm expend her yellow labours for
> thee? For thee does she undo herself?
>
> *Cyril Tourneur, c. 1575–1626*

There are all sorts of silences – as many perhaps as
there are textures to our sense of touch or shades of
color to the eye. But I will always remember the extraordinary silence that fell over a Pittsburgh courtroom
on October 13, 1995, when an African-American journalist and world-known author walked in slow motion,
his feet in chains, to present testimony in his own civil
suit against his prison (SCI Greene) and Pennsylvania's
Department of Corrections for violation of his human
rights. His name – Mumia Abu-Jamal.

Ripples of silence froze in his shackled footsteps. As if
on'a move waves could be stilled, this was a silence of
total paradox: the volatile, scarcely hidden presence of
loaded police weapons targeting the reined-in love of
members of the family in the courtroom – men, women,
and children who have been unable to touch him for

fourteen years. I was reminded of Coleridge's uncannily arrested sea: a spell cast against the forces of life. Having at last reached the stand in hi-tech noiselessness (America now produces *silent* chains for her prisoners' feet), a gentle giant spoke and was unbound by his own words.

The defense team for SCI Greene proceeded to interrogate Mumia, asking him repeatedly whether he knew he was violating prison rules when he wrote his book *Live From Death Row*. "Yes," quietly. (A tremor through the silence.) Did he know he was violating the same rules when he accepted payment for articles, commentaries, etc...? "Yes," in soft-spoken, vibrant tones. (The silence stirs.) Did he know that the current punishment for entering into "the illicit business of writing" behind bars was ninety days in the "hole" and a prison investigation justifying the monitoring of his mail and limited access to all categories of visitors including family, paralegals, spiritual counselors, the press? "Yes," patiently, wearily. (The silence vibrates but congeals again, oily and ominous.)

"Why then, if you knew, did you go ahead and write that book?"

"Because, whatever the cost to me, I knew I *had* to offer to the world a window into the souls of those who, like me, suffer barbaric conditions on America's death rows..."

American silence shattered like cheap glass. Judge
Benson suspended the hearing…

THE BOOK YOU ARE about to read, Mumia's second
"crime" since *Live From Death Row,* breaks through
American silence yet again as its author shares with us
his prison-brewed antidotes against bars of silence
more deadly than the cold steel he touches every day.

In the recent HBO-Channel 4-Otmoor documentary
Mumia Abu-Jamal: A Case for Reasonable Doubt?,
Mumia finds words to tell us about the inhuman experience of sensory isolation he has been exposed to for
two-thirds of a generation:

> Once someone closes that door, there is no
> sound. There is the sound of silence in your cell.
> There is the sound of an air-conditioner and the
> sound of silence, the sound you create in your
> own cell. The sense of isolation is all but total,
> because you're cut off even from the sonic pres-
> ence of people. Imagine going into your bath-
> room, locking the door behind you, and not
> leaving that bathroom, except for an hour or two
> [each day]…and staying in that bathroom for the
> rest of your natural life, with a date to die.

In *Death Blossoms*, Mumia's victories against such sensory deprivation are as many prizes he has wrested

from prison. ("Prize" and "prison" share the same root
meaning: "to seize.") However, he does not present us
with ready-made, do-it-yourself, take-away prescrip-
tions: that would be too simple. If a pattern of anti-
carceral antidotes is to be found in the pages that
follow, it is for *us* to learn how to detect them, just as
Henry James believed that readers need to reach a
certain stage of lucidity before they can make out the
hidden "figure" in a writer's "carpet."

Nothing, Mumia lets us know, can begin without the
word. Writing behind locked doors gives durable sound
to prison silence, spiritual distance from a madding
crowd of politicians and elected judges whose careers
are built on the blood of others, creative dimension to
the sound and fury of a world lost. In writing, there is a
renewed bonding: unshackled hands grasping note-
book, fingers touching pencil, pencil touching paper,
paper touched by readers who are in turn touched by
meaning. And *something* is badly needed to prevent
the outside world from receding, to arrest the slowing-
down of the metabolism of exchange with one's remembered community. Do colors pale and falter with
Plexiglas filtering? Is there a sepia-like transmutation
due to the overexposure of much revisited memories?

Death Blossoms seems bathed in a shimmering translu-
cency, as if remembered color 'n' sound are bleeding out
of prison-reality, and this existential hemorrhage can be

stopped only by the "brilliant etching of writing upon the brain."

CAN ALL THE CENTURIES of world philosophy even begin to visualize the dreams and nightmares of our death row inmates? The raw stuff of dreams draws on the immediacy of the sentient world – but when that world is suppressed, what happens to those dreaming processes which constitute one of the foundations of human sanity? Rollo May has written about that existential pain at the heart of all human exile: the inability to go home. Homelessness, like noiselessness and lack of physical contact, is at the core of American "correction." It is the experience of being at home or not, of being able to go home or not, that sustains the sense of self or begins to shatter it. And it is one of the amazing strengths of this book that Mumia has turned his mind into his home, showing us in the process how out-of-our-minds we may have become in the "open" society outside. Mumia's inner home is so limitless that when we exit this book, it is into our own materialistic, petty reality-cells that we enter, apparently of our own "free" will.

This is not classic autobiography or even "intellectual" biography. It is the narrative of an escape from prison into the liberated territory of the mind, a pacing not of the cage but of the psyche, a jogging not in the pen

but in the open space Mumia calls "reaching beyond."
We are privileged that he takes us with him on a liber-
ating tour of his own freedom. Resolutely on'a move
within his own spiritual quest, Mumia makes us understand that "free" men and women can imprison and
arrest their own revolutions just as "inmates" can set
free a boundless revolution of the mind. As Frantz
Fanon, the late psychiatrist and freedom-fighter, wrote
in his *Wretched of the Earth*, "Imperialism leaves behind
germs of rot which we must clinically detect and remove
from our land but from our minds as well."

Our minds are indeed bombarded with media hype and
racial stereotypes. Who does not recall the Disneyland
face of a womanchild tearfully describing (for prime-
time consumption) the black "monster" who murdered
her two small boys? Except that this killer turned out to
be the figment of her own homicidal imagination…Yet
how many Mumia Abu-Jamals were arrested or ha-
rassed before the truth was duly established? Who
does not remember a Boston-based Italian-American as
he testified, convincingly, to witnessing the murder of
his wife by a black "thug?" Except that this dark fiend
turned out to be a projection straight out of the
husband's criminal mind…But, meanwhile, how many
Abu-Jamals? Who can forget a tear-streaked widow
telling over and over again how the defendant (Mumia)
smiled diabolically as the prosecution showed the jury

the blood-stained shirt of her policeman-husband?
Except that the minutes of the trial prove that Judge
Sabo had barred Mumia from the courtroom that
day…And so the pattern repeats itself as we are told
that a certain Wesley Cook, a.k.a. Mumia Abu-Jamal,
killed a police officer who happened to be brutalizing
his brother. But who is the real Mumia beyond these
false, cold-blooded projections?

Death Blossoms is a personal *and* collective answer to
this question, a generous and human song of innocence for all the unseen, voiceless men and women
imprisoned by guilty stereotypes way before they set
foot in a penitentiary.

Predictably, another "invisible man" haunts this case:
he was seen running away from the scene of the
shooting by at least three witnesses (Dessie Hightower,
William Singletary, Veronica Jones), and all have since
spoken up concerning the police intimidation they
underwent simply for insisting that *this* man was not
a figment of their black folks' imagination…

ALTHOUGH MUMIA'S LIFE-FORCES are sealed off
and preyed upon by a carceral onslaught tantamount
to hi-tech slavery, he distills in these pages the ultimate
rebuttal of his imprisonment: mental and spiritual au-
tarchy.

Death Blossoms displays a deceptively simple meshing of form and content. In fact, one of the most fascinating figures in Mumia's "carpet" is quite literally the carpet itself, the weaving of a web of words. Revealingly, towards the end of the book, Norman, an inmate, marvels at a spider's defiance of prison rules as it spins its web under his sink. Mumia, who soon discovers a spider of his own, weaves anecdote into antidote, and we begin to see that the book we hold in our hands is also a web spun out of the creative threads of a mind-made home; just as Anansi, the spider of ancient African folklore, is the source of a life-web unraveled from within.

As is uncannily the case with much of Mumia's writing, the psychological truth is also borne out scientifically. Randy Lewis, a molecular biologist who has been studying spiders' secrets for years, has recently written that "spider silk absorbs more energy before it breaks than any other material on earth." The writing in *Death Blossoms* is as prison proof as the silk for vests, currently derived from imprisoned, anesthetized spiders, is bullet proof. And from his carceral lab, Mumia's word-threads reach through and beyond prison bars; they are symbols of the essential twine of bonding with those on the outside. Together they form a web which is an almost literal image for those "holes in the soul" he writes of. But the same web also healingly re-creates in prison the reality of "the whole connected web of nature" and holds us all together as a community in spite of the most brutal assaults. As he notes in reference to the bonds that unite his beloved brothers and sisters of MOVE even after numerous sinister, programmed attempts to destroy their community: "Using neither nails nor lumber, John Africa constructed from the fabric of the heart a tightly cohesive body."

Many of us will not emerge from this book unsnared, for to the extent that we cannot deny the knowledge of what we have read, we are faced with a vital question: Knowing what we know, having become witnesses, can we continue to live and let die?

DEATH BLOSSOMS raises the issue of the innocence of one man – any man – at the hands of an elitist society that manufactures and projects its guilt upon its citizens in order to enrich itself. I am reminded here of my father's character, Fred Daniels, in *The Man Who Lived Underground*. Pursued by the police for a crime he did not commit, Daniels is robbed of his innocence and escapes underground into the city's sewers to avoid capture. As he tries to survive in hiding by resorting to stealing, he takes to peering through cellar doors and invisibly watches others being robbed of *their* innocence as they are punished for *his* thefts. After an old watchman falsely accused on his account commits suicide, Daniels understands from the depths of his netherworld that we are *all* robbed of our innocence and are therefore *all* condemned to guilt. He emerges from the sewers with the urge to share this truth with the world:

> If he could show them what he had seen, then they would feel what he had felt, and they in turn would show it to others, and those others would feel as they had felt, and soon everybody would be governed by the same impulse of pity.

Similar threads of poignant hope and faith in justice run through *Death Blossoms,* making visible witnesses of us all. Veronica Jones, a hounded witness in Mumia's case, was moved by the same impulse when she recently came forward to set a false record straight, but she was arrested at the stand for sticking to the truth of what she saw – a man running away – and for courageously accepting the responsibility that goes with taking the truth out of the "underground"…

Our America, geographically so vast and rich, historically so young and green, has traditionally preferred the materialism of *space* to the invisible threads *time* spins through her landscapes and the experience of her restless peoples. Mumia's writing reconnects us with a much-needed sense of continuity, with the history of our birth as a people on western shores through the

Middle Passage, with our ensuing struggle down
through time, ongoing, on'a move.

For Mumia, a wholistic struggle – the warp and woof of
it – unfolds not only in terms of space-oriented interna-
tionalism, but also through the transgenerational glue
contained in the web parabole. It is sadly ironical,
though, that such an appreciation of the spiritual essence of time should come from a death row inmate
who lacks the material wealth that buys life-time in
America. But Mumia, with characteristic selflessness,
enjoins us to look beyond ourselves at the fragile
blooms of our children, and help them "dwell in the
house of tomorrow," where we may not be.

A BLOSSOM IS one of the life forms most bound up
with the message of time. The fruit it becomes holds in
its flesh the memory of the grand-bud that came before it, and the foretaste of its passage through rot.
According to the most haunting of blues, sung by the
sister with the eternal magnolia in her hair, there were
many "strange fruit" hanging from our southern trees.
But do our landscapes remember? According to legend, death flowers (also called "mandragore") grew
under innocent men who had swung high. These
blooms held wondrous powers of fertility and con-
tinuum in the hands of the damned of the earth.

As I was reading the manuscript of *Death Blossoms*, I received a deeply moving letter from Mumia recounting his grief at the violent death of Tupac Shakur – a Panther family child, a promising but unfulfilled cub nipped in the bud. "What loss!" Mumia writes. "The son of a Panther who never knew his mother's glory; who called himself a 'thug;' who never realized his truest self, his truest power." Mumia's words will strike a deep chord in those of us who have had to teach our children to become mental guerrillas, and to thread their way through the grim statistics of their own mortality. "Every two hours, one of you dies of gunshot wounds," we force ourselves to teach them.

MUMIA'S INABILITY to touch the grandchildren born to him while on death row is, microcosmically, a double bind experienced by far too many in our decaying "communities:" the intergenerational connections of life are eroded, foreshortened at both ends of our life-spans. Targeted by the FBI as a child, Mumia cannot bond with his own children, or theirs – and all have been robbed. My father, Richard Wright, would have met my children and theirs, had he not died in his prime, in unelucidated circumstances. Our generations are torn asunder and brushed aside like cobwebs; they are cut off and isolated – as if on their own death row.

Over half a century after *Native Son*, Bigger – my paper brother – still haunts America, because in his premature death at the hands of the State, there was a foretaste of coming rot. Tupac? Another real-life native son in the long chain since decimation. We live and breathe this state of recurrent loss! We need to be able to find the right rites to mourn so many thousands gone, if only to prevent the next ones from going. Because those slain in childhood will have no children…

It is a healing strength of this book that Mumia, who lives at such mortal risk, can hand us the connective strands of a net to throw far over the great divide, towards generations of children we may never get to know or see or touch. But as he makes clear, we can love them ahead, preventively. And maybe this bond-net, flung far across time as a love Supreme, will keep them from going too unfortified, too gentle into the bad night of renewed bondage.

Baudelaire's *Les Fleurs du Mal* and Wilde's *Ballad of Reading Gaol* are prime examples of forbidden works written and banned at the end of the nineteenth century, only to become universally loved in the twentieth.

And so here are Mumia Abu-Jamal's *Death Blossoms* – timelessly.

Paris
October 1996

Steve Wiser

The corridors leading to death row at SCI Greene, Pennsylvania's state-of-the-art supermax, are spanking new. Floor tiles gleam like glass; off-white block walls blend with steel blue window frames and hand rails; smells of wax and lemon-scented detergents permeate the hallways. Even the germs are killed. It's like a hospital – except for one thing: the absence of humanity.

Electronic devices control and monitor every human motion. Cleverly concealed video cameras beam silently from every angle, small speakers crackle in concrete walls. From behind thick glass panels, uniformed guards follow each step. It is enough to make one feel naked, for – literally – the very walls have eyes and ears.

At the end of the long, empty passage is a set of double, remotely-controlled doors; beyond them a bleak guard station serves as the command center of L-5. It is the epicenter of this industrial edifice. Yet here one comes face to face with what the system tries hardest to conceal: humanity. Humanity, in all its warmth, richness, and earthiness.

I first met Mumia Abu-Jamal in May, 1995. I had no idea what to expect. I had visited numerous prisons before, from Bastille-like fortresses in Great Britain to Nigerian hell-holes where (instead of razor wire) the walls were lined with vultures, their hideous shriveled heads peering this way and that. But I had never been to a death house.

DEATH ROW WAS A SHOCK. But I was even less prepared to meet the man I had come to visit there: a tall, athletically-built African-American whose *joie de vivre* filled his tiny visiting compartment and seemed to overflow, through the Plexiglas partition separating us, into mine. Sitting there opposite him, I discovered a brilliant, compassionate, hearty, articulate man – a man of rare character, tempered and profoundly deepened by suffering.

From the outset, Mumia and I found ourselves communicating heart to heart. To a passing guard, it must have been a strange sight: two cell-mates, as it were – one a bald, white minister from a religious order, the other an African-American inmate whose long dreadlocks and urban savvy betrayed an entirely different background.

Even more strange was our discovery of the common values and viewpoints shared by our spiritual families – Mumia's beloved brothers and sisters in the MOVE Organization, and my fellow members of the Bruderhof, a community movement grounded in New Testament teachings. The more we learned about each other, the closer we felt.

As my weekly visits to Mumia continued, all of us at the Bruderhof became increasingly aware of the blatant injustices of his trial – and increasingly active in the international campaign to protest his death sentence. We joined rallies, wrote to government officials and newspaper editors, and printed his writings in our journal, *The Plough*. Not surprisingly, we were met with plenty of criticism, and many who had previously claimed to be our friends censured us for "meddling" in such radical "politics." On the other hand, we gained hundreds of new friends, including death row inmates, writers, artists, and rappers, social workers, teachers, activists, and other religious and secular groups who stand in opposition to the death penalty. We have been deeply enriched by our contact with Mumia.

Our involvement, of course, was spurred on by far more than Mumia's case *per se:* our church has always spoken out against individual and state-sanctioned violence – from the treatment of Jews in Nazi Germany to the bombing of Vietnam and Iraq. Yet even without the historical precedents, we could not have remained silent. Why? Because the life of an innocent man is at stake.

Mumia is, in reality, a prisoner of conscience. Long before his arrest in 1981 – from his teen years in the Black Panther Party to his career as a radio journalist – his commitment to the ideals of honesty and fairness, and his tireless attempts to unmask the lie of governmental "justice," cost him his freedom. Tragically, they may cost him his life.

Punished most recently for writing a book – his controversial exposé *Live from Death Row* (Addison-Wesley, 1994) – Mumia is painfully aware of how quickly the broadest civil liberties in the world are curtailed when political power is at stake. Still, he continues to speak out. And as his fellow human beings – as his brothers and sisters – we have felt it a matter of conscience to assist him in bringing to the printed page his thoughts and feelings. In this way, from out of the sterile steel-and-block walls that isolate him, blossoms have unfolded – blossoms of thought and of spirit. Penned beneath the scribbled symbol of a flower and referred to by the silent gesture of cupped hands – wrists shackled, but palms uplifted to unfurl the fingers – they have now drifted far beyond the confines of the prison fence.

I have visited Mumia as his "spiritual advisor" for eighteen months now. There have been days when I entered the "row" depressed, weighed down with those petty problems that plague all of us at one time or another. Yet I have left again deeply refreshed and strengthened.

How is it that a well-spring of life can arise on death row? That a condemned man can speak – sincerely, even effusively – of the "wonder and joy of Life?" How is it that a despised convict, locked in a cell the size of a bathroom in the most godforsaken spot in Pennsylvania, can imbue with a spirit of freedom those who are "free?"

MUMIA IS SIMPLY A MAN. Writing to me last summer from a sweltering prison block near Philadelphia, thirteen dreadful days before his scheduled (and then suddenly postponed) execution date, his soul cries out:

> I would be lying if I told you I've not had those nights – dark nights of the soul where death itself seems welcome. I sometimes want to shout – "I am not a symbol; I am a man!" But on this my fabled "voice" falters. I am no more, no less, than a man – a human fighting for his breath in a shifting sea of codified hatred. As I seek a safe shore, a harbor, I am buffeted by swells that threaten to drown out my very existence…For me, the "law" is not a refuge, but a ravenous great whale circling ever closer, seeking its prey.

And so he sits on death row today, his future uncertain, but his spirit still unfettered. As he writes in another letter:

…Loneliness is but an illusion. One man, "living" on one of the most damned sites on earth, is not truly alone. The death chambers of America are not as tightly sealed as many may suspect, for how can Spirit be kept out?

It is often said that when a writer bares his soul in a book, a small part of it travels to every reader. Here, then, from the heart and soul of Mumia Abu-Jamal to yours, are the flowers of his spirit.

New Meadow Run Bruderhof
October 1996

A Write-up for Writing

ON JUNE 3, 1995, one day after being served with a death warrant, I was served with a "write-up," a misconduct report for "engaging actively in a business or profession," i.e., as a journalist. So strongly does the State object to me writing what you are now reading that they have begun to punish me, while I'm in the most punitive section that the system allows, for daring to speak and write the truth.

The institutional offense? My book, *Live from Death Row.* It paints an uncomplimentary picture of a prison system that calls itself "correctional" but does little more than corrupt human souls; a system that eats hundreds of millions of dollars a year to torture, maim, and mutilate tens of thousands of men and women; a system that teaches bitterness and hones hatred.

Clearly, what the government wants is not just death, but silence. A "correct" inmate is a silent one. One who speaks, writes, and exposes horror for what it is, is given a "misconduct." Is that a correct system? A system of corrections? In this department of state government, the First Amendment is a nullity. It doesn't apply.

No one – not a cop, nor a guard – can find one lie in *Live from Death Row;* indeed, it is precisely because of its truth that it is a target of the state and its minions – a truth they don't want you to see.

Consider: Why haven't you seen, heard, or read anything like this on TV, radio, or in the papers? Newspapers, radio, and TV are increasingly the property of multinational corporations or wealthy individuals and therefore reflect the perspective of the rich and the established, not the poor and powerless.

In *Live from Death Row,* you hear the voices of the many, the oppressed, the damned, and the bombed. I paid a high price to bring it to you, and I will pay more; but, I tell you, I would do it a thousand times, no matter what the cost, because it is right! To quote John Africa;

"When you are committed to doing what is right, the power of righteousness will never betray you…" It was right to write *Live from Death Row,* and it's right for you to read it, no matter what cop, guard, prisoncrat, politician, or media mouthpiece tells you otherwise.

Every day of your life, no doubt, you've heard of "freedom of speech" and "freedom of the press." But what can such "freedom" mean without the freedom to read, or to hear, what you want?

As you read this, know that I am being punished by the government for writing *Live from Death Row,* and for writing these very words. Indeed, I've been punished by the United States government for my writings since I was fifteen years of age – but I've kept right on writing. **You keep right on reading!**

BOOKS

A N D T H E S T A T E

The writer who is endorsed by the State is the writer who says what everyone wants to hear: the allowable things. It is noteworthy that even at this time in world history, those who write satire, social commentary, or works of opinion can be damned, threatened, and marked for death because of their words. Take Salman Rushdie. How many people have actually read his works? I have read *The Satanic Verses*, also *Haroun and the Sea of Stories*. I cannot speak for a Muslim, of course, yet I found him fascinating, funny, and an extremely good writer. I can understand why the State felt threatened by his work. What I don't understand is why they would think of doing something that will only immortalize it.

If there's one thing we've learned in two thousand years, it's that you cannot kill a book. One of the greatest science-fiction films I have ever seen, *Fahrenheit 451* (that's the point at which paper combusts spontaneously), which is based on a Ray Bradbury novel, portrays a futuristic society in which books are banned and people cannot hold unorthodox ideas. In this society there are subversives – people who read books. The subversives keep their books hidden in attics, in basements, and behind false walls. And this

old lady in the film tells a young girl that she likes books
and has some hidden in her attic. Somehow the word
gets out, and when it does, the alarms start ringing
and they call the fire department. The fire brigade
rushes to the house, axes the doors, and starts
a fire: they burn the house to the ground.
Finally all the subversives or rebels flee
the country to a place where people
become books.

In a sense, the film tries to
show how far the State
will go to ban books, or
anything it perceives to be
dangerous, for that matter.
But it also shows how useless
all those measures are.

You cannot kill a book.

Capit🏛l
Punishment

THE DEATH PENALTY is a creation of the State, and politicians justify it by using it as a stepping stone to higher political office. It's very popular to use isolated cases – always the most gruesome ones – to make generalizations about inmates on death row and justify their sentences. Yet it is deceitful; it is untrue, unreal. Politicians talk about people on death row as if they are the worst of the worst, monsters and so forth. But they will not talk about the thousands of men and women in our country serving lesser sentences for similar and even identical crimes. Or others who, by virtue of their wealth and their ability to retain a good private lawyer, are not convicted at all. The criminal court system calls itself a justice system, but it measures privilege, wealth, power, social status, and – last but not least – race to determine who goes to death row.

Why is it that Pennsylvania's African-Americans, who make up only 9% of its population, comprise close to two-thirds of its death row population?[1] It is because its largest city, Philadelphia, like Houston and Miami and other cities, is a place where politicians have built their careers on sending people to death row. They are not

---

[1] See Abu-Jamal, *Live from Death Row,* xvii.

making their constituents any safer. They are not administering justice by their example. They are simply revealing the partiality of justice.

Let us never forget that the overwhelming majority of people on death row are poor. Most of them cannot afford the resources to develop an adequate defense to compete with the forces of the State, let alone money to buy a decent suit to wear in court. As the O.J. Simpson case illustrated once again, the kind of defense you get is the kind of defense you can afford. In Pennsylvania, New Jersey, and New York, in Florida, in Texas, in Illinois, in California – most of the people on death row are there because they could not afford what O.J. could afford, which is the best defense.

One of the most widespread arguments in favor of the death penalty is that it deters crime. Study after study has shown that it does not. If capital punishment deters anything at all, it is rational thinking. How else would it be conceivable in a supposedly enlightened, democratic society? Until we recognize the evil irrationality of capital punishment, we will only add, brick by brick, execution by execution, to the dark temple of Fear. How many more lives will be sacrificed on its altar?

RECENTLY I CAME across words from Gibran, one of my boyhood heroes, and reflected on them as I hadn't in more than a generation. What reader of this passage from *The Prophet* can but pause for thought?

Oftentimes have I heard you speak of one who commits a wrong as though he were not one of you, but a stranger unto you and an intruder upon your world.

But I say that even as the holy and the righteous cannot rise beyond the highest which is in each one of you,

So the wicked and the weak cannot fall lower than the lowest which is in you also.

And as a single leaf turns not yellow but with the silent knowledge of the whole tree,

So the wrong-doer cannot do wrong without the hidden will of you all.

Like a procession you walk together towards your god-self.

You are the way and the wayfarers.

And when one of you falls down he falls for those behind him, a caution against the stumbling stone.

Ay, and he falls for those ahead of him, who though faster and surer of foot, yet removed not the stumbling stone.

Here I sat, on death row, of all places, and not only on death row, but on Phase II, beside men who, like me, had a few weeks left to live.

One of them, a middle-aged, frog-voiced Vietnam vet,
would rather die, than live in this Hell of cells, and, refus-
ing all appeals, did die by lethal injection; by judicial
murder, by state diktat. His name was Leon Moser.

Two doors down from me, I tried to get him to fight for
his life, to get him to battle the political whores who
were using his life, and his very death, as stepping
stones to higher political office such as elected judgeship:

"Look, man. I understand how you feel. Hell, if I was a
middle-aged white dude from the boondocks stuck down
here in this black 'n' Spanish village, well – hey – I might
do the same thing, or feel like it. Graterford must make
you feel as if you were in a foreign country.

"Also, wouldn't it be good to beat those slimy lawyers
in the D.A.'s office, who owe their careers to your life –
and your death? I know you hate lawyers!"

"I think lawyers are sleazy, yes. But I don't really care
about being executed. As far as I'm concerned the man
they sentenced to death died over ten years ago. To
execute me won't mean nothing, 'cause that man ain't
alive no more. To kill me, Jamal, is just like puttin' out
garbage."

Moser welcomed death like a long-lost lover, and the
State, thirsty for his blood, rushed him off into eternity,
ignoring even the attempted telephonic intercession of

Remembering Moser

a federal judge. Defense lawyers criticized his execution as a rush to death.

In those few times I saw him in that dark, humid, and stifling Phase II, Moser appeared fifteen years older than he really was; his hair more white than brown, his beard a whitened, chest-long brush, his visage a stark contrast to pictures published in the daily press, which showed a younger, browner-haired, less furtive face.

He walked with a permanent hump, as if a demon the size of a rogue elephant rode his back, bending him down, down, and still farther down.

For such a one, might not death bring the hope of a respite?

James Harris

POLITICS

PEOPLE SAY they don't care about politics; they're not involved or don't want to get involved, but they are. Their involvement just masquerades as indifference or inattention. It is the silent acquiescence of the millions that supports the system. When you don't oppose a system, your silence becomes approval, for it does nothing to interrupt the system. People use all sorts of excuses for their indifference. They even appeal to God as a shorthand route for supporting the status quo. They talk about law and order. But look at the system, look at the present social "order" of society. Do you see God? Do you see law and order? There is nothing but disorder, and instead of law there is only the illusion of security. It is an illusion because it is built on a long history of injustices: racism, criminality, and the enslavement and genocide of millions. Many people say it is insane to resist the system, but actually, it is insane *not* to.

The Search

LIFE HAS EVER BEEN in search of answers to basic questions – What is Life? Who is God? Why?

As a boy, this quest took me to the oddest places. When Mama dragged us to church, it seemed more for her solace, than ours. A woman who spent most of her life in the South, she must've felt tremendous social coldness up North. "Down home" was "down South," for even after over a decade, the brick and concrete jungle we walked daily didn't seem like home.

Only at church did it seem that Mama returned home. It was a refuge where women her age sought a few hours for the soul's rest while the preacher performed. In a sense, Sunday trips to church were her weekly "homegoing." They were islands of the South – its camaraderie, its rhythms, its spiritual community – come north.

Yet for myself, as for most of my siblings, church was a foreign affair. We had never lived (and seldom visited) in Mama's southern birthland, and the raucous, tambourine-slapping, sweat-drenched, organ-pounding milieu couldn't be more alien. We weren't southerners.

Black preachers, especially those of southern vintage, are extroverts in style, diction, and cadence. They may yell, shriek, hum, harrumph, or sing. Some strut the stage. Some dance. Black Baptist preachers, especially, are never dull or monotonal. Their sermons aren't particularly cerebral. Nor should they be. They preach to congregations whose spirits have been beaten down and battered all week long. To them, Sundays are thus days when the spirit, not the mind, needs lifting. So preachers must perform, and sermons become exercises in exuberance.

I remember staring at the preacher – his furrowed face shining with perspiration, eyes closed, lips locked in a holy grimace – and wondering to myself, "What da hell did he just say?" His thick, rich, southern accent, so accessible to Mama, was Greek to me.

Part of me was embarrassed, but the other couldn't give a damn. I couldn't care less what the preacher was saying, and he couldn't care less what I was thinking. I was thinking: I am bored to tears.

The only "salvation" I felt in church was the rapturous joy I felt when I looked around me. Here, I thought, are some of the most beautiful girls in the world.

I was lost in a reverie, in rapt adoration, my eyes locked on a girl a few pews back. She had fresh pressed hair; a crisp, starched dress; patent leather shoes that shone brighter than the real stuff. Her dark brown legs shimmered with the luster of Vaseline…

Then a painful pluck would pull me from my rapture, and Mama's clenched lips whispered, "Boy! Turn yo' narrow behind around now! Straighten up!" I would simmer. Who would choose to stare at an old preacher when there was a pretty girl to look at? If I hadda choice between 'em – well, that wouldn't be no contest. But I was only ten. Mama made the choice for me. I turned, glowering.

It was only several years later, when I was no longer forced to go to church, that I really began to explore the realm of the spirit. Sometimes I went to Dad's church. Although Mama was a bred-in-the-bone Baptist, Dad was Episcopalian. He had taught me how to read by using the Bible, and seemed to take pleasure in listening to me read Holy Scripture.

After the raucousness of Mama's Baptist church, Dad's Episcopalianism seemed its quiet antithesis. Whereas Second Pilgrim's was cramped, Episcopal was spacious. Baptists sang and danced; Episcopalians were reserved and stately. Mama's friends shook their tambourines in North Philly. Dad's sang hymns in the foreign outlands of Southwest Philly.

Dad's church was vast, reflecting substance and wealth,
yet it didn't feel like home. Maybe Mama's church was a
sweatbox. Dad's seemed a cold fortress. Soon I began to
seek my own spirit-refuge, going wherever I felt the
spirit lead me. Like to the synagogue.

THROUGH READING the Bible and other books, I
knew that the Scriptures were supposed to be the Word
of God. I thus reasoned that among the Jews, whose
faith is rooted in the Old Testament, I would find this
Word in a purer form. One day I went to seek it.

In North Philly's bustling black and Puerto Rican neighborhoods, Jews were a distinct and rare minority   old
men, and a few women, who sold chickens, clothing, or
peanuts. Their house of prayer, however, was hardly
distinct: a small synagogue, it stood recessed, tucked in
between the storefronts that margined it like the edges
of a book cover.

Inside the vestibule, six or seven old men stood, chant-
ing in an unknown tongue. They wore yarmulkes on
their heads, and prayer shawls fastened across their
chests covered their stooped shoulders. The room was
dark, and what little sun seeped in hardly penetrated the
dimness. Dust motes swam like goldfish in thin ribbons

of filtered light. To this day, I remember the dust; the dust of old stones, of old men. And the smell of old men.

The rabbi, his eyes enlarged by bifocals, shuffled over to me, his shoulders stooped, his eyes sharp. "Can I help you, young man?" His speech was guttural, thick; colored with Yiddishisms. There seemed to be – or was I only imagining it? – an aura of fear around him stirred, perhaps, by my entrance. Who was this big, beardless youth confronting him?

As tall black men learn to do, I made myself mentally smaller, and looked askance as I explained my reason for entering the synagogue.

"Yes, sir. I – umm – I'm – umm…I wanna learn about Judaism."
"Vy iz dat?"
"Well, I'm interested in learning about the religion that really began Christianity."
"Vell – Vy?"
"Umm…becuz I think I wanna become a Jew."
"Dyou *vat?* Vat you mean? Vy dyou say *dat?*"
"Well – I'm interested in a pure religion. I've read that the Bible has been tampered with; there are different translations and stuff. I wanna study what God really said, you know…"

The rabbi stared at me. He was trying to formulate an answer, but the words stuck to his tongue. I looked into his eyes and saw incredulity dueling with quiet surprise. Is he serious? silly? he seemed to be asking. Then he turned and looked around, as if searching for something.

"Vait uh minute."

"Zis vill help you, young man," he said, handing me an envelope, and walking me to the door.

"Ven you are finished, come back, ya?"

"Thank you, sir!"

"By ze vay, dyou know, zair ah black Chews. Haf you efer heard von Sammy Davis chunior?"

I nodded assent.

"Vell, he is a black Chew, you know?"

He bade me farewell. I left the Market Street Synagogue high with expectation, racing home.

Once in my room, I tore apart the thick brown envelope and found a slim, rust-colored volume bound in leather. I opened it, but stopped short in dismay. What was this? There was not one English word within its covers! It was entirely in Hebrew. Tears leapt to my eyes. The search was sure to continue.

III

MY FIRST VISIT to a Catholic church was a visit into a place of contrasts, a place where the visages in stone radiated reverence, but faces of flesh reflected unmitigated hatred.

I remember sitting in Mass, listening to the strange intonations of the priests – *Agnus Dei, qui tollis peccata mundi...miserere nobis.* – and noticing their turned heads, faces tight with spirals of hatred, aimed at me, a lanky black youth kneeling in the white midst.

"Do they know me?" I wondered. "Why are they angry at me?"

Confusion warred with amazement: how could the House of God so plainly be a house of hatred toward one who sought the divine presence within its walls? Wasn't this the Church Universal, the Mother Church?

Although barely in my teens, I knew what I saw, and I acknowledged the feelings of the people around me. Matronly heads covered in firmly-knotted scarves, these silent, solid, middle-aged Poles, Ukrainians, and Slavs (there were also a few Puerto Ricans) never said a thing, but their faces – their coldly darting eyes, and tight, wrinkled mouths – spoke to me louder than screams:

"Nigger! What are you doing in this church? *Our* church?"

Day by day, week by week, month by month, I began to ask myself that very question.

Where once the church had offered a quiet place for spiritual reflection on its catechismal mysteries, it now pulsated with resentment at my dark presence.

When I went to catechism I heard of one world; when I walked into church I saw another.

The straw of severance came on April 4, 1968, the day Martin Luther King, Jr. was assassinated. I was on my way to catechism, and as I trudged my way to the rectory, my slowing gait seemed to reflect my inner reluctance. A weight hung on my mind like an anvil.

"King believed in nonviolence – and *still* they killed him!"

"They? Who *they?*"

"White folks – white folks couldn't bear to hear him – to see him!"

My conversation with self went point-counter-point… By the time I got off the trolley near St. John's, my legs were leaden. I walked at a snail's pace.

Sitting down with Father to begin the lesson, he noticed my reticence.

"What's wrong, young man? You seem distracted."

"Father…"

"Yes, go on."

"I heard on the news today that Reverend Martin Luther King was assassinated…"

"I heard it too. Some of the Fathers and brothers are glad."

"Glad?"

"Yes. They saw him as a troublemaker."

"Really? Really, Father?"

"Some – not all. Especially not one of our Fathers."

"Why 'especially' not one?"

"Well – how do I put it…Well – one of our Fathers is half-Negro."

"Really, Father?"

"Yes. Why?"

"Do you think I could talk to him?"

"Why?"

"Well, Father – perhaps…maybe he can understand how I feel."

"That may be, but, uh…you cannot talk with him."

"Why not, Father?"

"Well…it's a secret. I can't tell you which Father it is."

A man, a priest, ashamed of his race? I had come to catechism that night seeking peace for the tempest that raged in my soul. Now, leaving St. John's, I was more at sea than when I arrived.

All those months! A half-black priest! Ashamed of his

race? Priests who were *glad* that King was killed? Where was I? What was I doing here? I wept bitter tears. Not for King – I felt he was wrong, a soft-hearted non-realist – but for my parents and all others who revered him. King was an educated preacher of nonviolence, yet to these priests he was just another nigger.

What was I doing in this place, a place that hailed his murder? If they thought that way about him, how did they really feel about me?

I cried for the loss my mother and her generation felt – the assassination of their dreams, the scuttling of their barely-born hopes. I cried for the loss of a boy's faith. I cried for a nation on the razor's edge of chaos.

A BLACK NATIONALIST even in my pre-Black Panther youth, it was perhaps inevitable that my search for meaning would bring me, sooner or later, to test the waters at a local mosque. Little more than a storefront on an out-of-the-way street in South Philly, the building seemed the antithesis of all the religious sites I'd been to before. Christian and Jewish houses of worship were ornate as a rule, especially their cathedrals. This place could not have been plainer: walls painted white, with the front of the room adorned by a chalkboard that faced the assembled. There was also a flag featuring a white star and crescent in a bright field of red, with a letter in each corner: F, J, E, and I – Freedom, Justice, Equality, and Islam.

It was a summer night and mid-week, so the gathering was small, yet Brother Minister, a dark-skinned man in navy suit, glasses, and bow tie who went by the name of – was it Benjamin? Benjamin X? – preached passionately. The captive audience punctuated his every sentence: "Uh-huh!" "That's it!" "Teach, bro minister! Wake 'em up!" His baritone was smooth, colored by that ubiquitous southern accent I was to find later in almost every mosque I visited, whether north or south of the Mason-Dixon Line. His message was not.

"Brotha...I say to you here and now, the white man is the devil! Why, when you look at how this man has stolen millions of our people from Africa, sold our mothers and fathers into slavery in the hells of North America for four hundred years; beat us, abused us, lynched us, and tortured us – well, how could any man be anything *but* a devil?"

"Uh-huh!"

"Preach it, Bro. Minister!"

"Our leader and teacher, the Honorable Elijah Muhammad, teaches us, brotha, that the devil's time is almost over!"

"That's it, brotha!"

"Wake 'em up!"

"I said, 'The devil's time is almost up!' Why, look all around the world – from Vietnam to Detroit – and you'll see the white man catching hell! Am I right, brothas?"

"That's it!"

"Uh-huh!"

Minister Benjamin X spoke for what seemed to be hours, and after his lecture, a collection was taken.

Returning home, I reflected on the similarities between my Baptist and Muslim experiences. I was struck by how the Muslim minister – though his mouth vibrated with the rhythms and cadences of the black South, and though his message was shaped in a way that spoke to my ethnic, historical, and cultural realities – sounded for the most part like a Christian in a bow-tie.

The main difference, perhaps, lay in their views of evil. Where the Baptist spoke of a metaphysical devil, the Muslim preached of a living one. I couldn't bring myself to believe that the white man was supernatural, even supernaturally evil – if anything, they were sub-naturally human, I thought to myself. Yet it seemed as improbable that they were devils, as gods. The search would continue.

Thoughts on the Divine

An interviewer once asked the Mahatma Gandhi: "Gandhi-ji, it seems that you worship sometimes in temples, sometimes in churches, sometimes in mosques. What is your own religion?" Gandhi replied: "Follow me for a few days. Watch what I do; how I walk, what I say, and how I conduct myself generally. *That* is my religion."

THERE ARE AS MANY religions as there are cultures, and equally many names for the divine presence that is the heart of each. The energizing influence of belief keeps them apart, for to each adherent they contain truth that, from his or her perspective, is the *only* truth. All the same, it seems they flow in one direction, like many streams seeking release into one mighty river.

My youthful search for meaning revealed that no matter how differently the Infinite was clothed in the garb of a certain religion, it was there. In each, I found a new perception of the greatest good, that is, a belief in God or some other personification of the divine principle. I found, as George Bernard Shaw puts it, that there is "only one religion, though there are a hundred versions of it."

In Judaism, the ancient ancestral warrior is revered as all-powerful Yahweh, or Jehovah; to Christians, the Jewish carpenter Yeshuah is God yet also Man; for the Muslim, the ancient Meccan gods find fusion in one supreme being – *Al-Lah,* the God. In Hinduism, Lord Krishna emerges from a vast pantheon of ancient deities as a blue-black god who twirls and leaps in an eternal sacred dance. To the Buddhist, the insights of Gautama Siddhartha form the central core of a faith that holds the promise of enlightenment and the discovery of the true Self. In Santería, Condoblé, and Voudoun, the ancient gods of African antiquity have survived to smile behind the faces of the Catholic saints.

In the essence of each religion, then, we see a projection of the greatest good. For a threatened, nomadic desert tribe, what greater good than the worship of a mighty and powerful ancestor, a prominent warrior – Yahweh – who defended the clans? For the maligned followers of a Nazarethan carpenter, one crucified by the mightiest Empire of the age, why not the greater good of his victory over the tomb? For contentious Arab clans who saw each other through the lens of enmity and conflict, why

not the clarity and simplicity of One God to reign over
the throngs who crowd the K'aaba – One God to bring
unity to a people, a region, a sphere of influence?

To Hindus, whose plethora of deistic personalities reflect
the God-force that permeates all creation, Krishna – the
beautiful, playful, dark boy-god who loves cattle and
dances with other cowherds – turns the boring and mun-
dane into a sacred act. For the Buddhist, Gautama's
attainment of enlightenment seeks the void beyond
which no personality, human nor divine, exists. It be-
speaks a greater good that sees past the soul to ultimate
nothingness, a spiritual place of rest.

To millions of stolen and enslaved African peasants, for
whom return to the grasslands, forests, and villages of
the black motherland was physically impossible, their
religion was the only means of a voyage home. Under a
new, cooler sky, ancient gods and honored ancestors
came to life once more and provided the greater good of
spiritual survival, of an inner Self that could withstand the
most dehumanizing assaults and empower the soul to
remain sane. Even in the midst of a powerless existence,
the world of the invisible pulsed with names like
Yemonja, the goddess of the river; Obatala, chief of the
gods; and Shango, the god of war and thunder.

Many of our ideas about God and religions simply mirror
the traditions we have inherited from our forebears. They

are imbibed with mother's milk, openly, uncritically,
freely – illogical human expressions, exercises in irrationality. Others are perceptions gained only by leaping into
the dark arms of faith. God comes, in various faces, and
numerous personalities, depending on our myriad perceptions, needs, and histories. Yet if there are any
miracles left, it is that **GOD IS ONE.**

Night of Power

IN ISLAM, during the holy month of Ramadan, it is said that one night is holiest of all: *al Qadr*, the Night of Power. According to Islamic belief, it was on this night that the *Qu'ran* was delivered to the Prophet Mohammed, and it is thus the holiest of all nights. On this night, prayers are granted "for everything that matters."

The Night of Power is so deeply in-grained in the Muslim heart that a short chapter in the *Qu'ran* is devoted to it. It begins, as do all chapters therein, with the exclamation, "In the Name of God, the Compassionate, the Merciful," and goes on thus:

Verily we have sent this
In the Night of Power.

And what will convey to you
What the Night of Power is?

The Night of Power is better
Than a thousand months:

The Angels and the Spirit descend in it,
By permission of their Lord,
For everything that matters.

It is Peace:
This until the rise of daybreak.

I will never forget the Night of Power that shook me, not during the holy month of Ramadan, but in the hot, humid summer of 1995, when I sat on death row's Phase II with a date to die.

The sun had set behind the hills of West Virginia amid ominous thunderheads, and now the forces of nature struck like a divine assault team.

Lightning stabbed the earth as if in the throes of celestial passion, and so powerful were the bolts that the lights in the block – indeed, the whole jail – flickered out.

On Phase II, lights are kept burning twenty-four hours a day – bright during the day, dim at night – though in fact "dim" at two in the morning is hardly less than bright at noon. Tonight – for now at least – it was completely dark.

I sat on the cool metal table and looked out into the
night. Cell lights, hall lights, yard lights, black lights,
perimeter lights, and lights on poles had died, and
not even stars broke the black carpet. So dark!

Then: a splash of illumination that bathed the hills in
blue light, a rolling boom-BOOM of thunder, and a rapid
procession of blinks as lights went out all over the prison
complex.

It happened again and again and again, and yet
again – one sinuous bolt of lightning after the next
forking the black sky, then white-washing it to midday
brilliance for the brief space of an eye-blink.

I sat there in the first real darkness since my arrival to
Phase II, transfixed by the display of such raw, primeval
power. The strikes seemed so close, I felt the hair on
my arms rise.

The storm moved westward, over the prison and across
the hills, and in its magnificent wake, darkness reigned
as man's lights bowed their mechanical heads to the
power it had unleashed.

There I sat in the darkness, with less than a month to
live, yet I felt better than any other night I spent on
Phase II. I felt better even than I did a few weeks later,
the night my stay was granted. Why?

Then it dawned on me, like bright writing etched in my brain:

"Here is true power, my son.
See how easily it overwhelms man's 'power'?"

Watching the veins of nature pulse through the night sea of air, making – if only for milliseconds – daylight over the hills, I felt renewed. How puny man seemed before this divine dance!

I saw, then, that though human powers sought to strangle and poison me and those around me, they were powerless. I saw that there is a Power that makes man's power pale. It is the power of Love; the power of God, the power of Life. I felt it surging through every pore.

Nature's power prevailed over the man-made, and I felt, that night, that I would prevail. I would overcome the State's efforts to silence and kill me.

America exists

in a virtual sea of materialism. Here, one sees material excess in the midst of utter poverty. Here, in the cradle of global capital power, one finds more food, more clothing, more creature comforts, more material wealth than almost anywhere on this planet.

Ironically, the lives of many surrounded by opulence are awash in unhappiness. This nation eats most of the world's food. It consumes most of the world's energy. It treats the vast lands and seas of the earth as if it were a toilet bowl. It gains its material wealth from the theft of other people's lands and the exploitation of other people's labor.

Its principle is not – and never has been – something as amorphous as "Christianity"; it is naked materialism. This materialism drives not only the elite, but average, so-called everyday folk. It forms a perspective that permeates our entire society.

Even in the realm of sexuality we are, to paraphrase the singer Madonna, material girls and boys. We define ourselves by projections, the most variant quality in human personality.

If a man is born a male, but utilizes the latest biomedical technology to transform himself into a woman, is he a woman? Or is he rather a sexual materialist who has merely purchased a new sexual persona? Are we what we look like on the outside, or are we our biological functions?

As we are with our bodies, so we are with our environment. Consciously and unconsciously, directly and indirectly, by express intent and by oblique accident, we transform the natural world toward ends we neither know nor care to know.

We rape our Mother, Earth, for new toys to play with, in order to maximize profits for men already richer than Croesus. How much is enough?

If material things are not our salvation, why do we spend our energies in endless acquisition? If wealth makes us more cruel, more calloused, and colder, what is its good?

To be sure, we live in a material universe. We must eat, and we must drink of this earth's substance. Yet after we squander its resources and make it uninhabitable, will we be able, even with our material wealth, to restore the air, to reanimate our earth, to repair the genetic damage we have done?

We are greedily eating the very heart of our tomorrow and our children's tomorrows. And meanwhile our god – the dark force of international corporate power – decides, hour by hour, how destructive the day's economic engine will be; how much long-term gain will be destroyed in the race for short-term profit.

Life's

R E L I G I O N

We northerners are undoubtedly descended from barbarian races, also in respect to our talent for religion: we have little talent for it.

Supposing one were able to view the strangely painful and at the same time coarse and subtle comedy of European Christianity with the mocking and unconcerned eye of an Epicurean god, I believe there would be no end to one's laughter and amazement: for does it not seem that one will has dominated Europe for eighteen centuries, the will to make of man a sublime abortion?

Friedrich Nietzsche, *Beyond Good and Evil*

ONE MIGHT be both accused and excused of hyperbole if one were to assert that God has been utilized to justify more human evil than has Satan. Yet dozens of philosophers (not only Nietzsche) have pointed out that whatever its origins and promises, the reality of religion is this: it has often been less a force for liberation than a tool of oppression – an impetus for civil unrest, warfare and genocide.

Wherever one stands on the religion divide, it seems
clear that a new, life-affirming spirit needs expression
as we end a century of carnage and move into a new
millennium. Our supposedly enlightened age – the Modern Century – opened with the Boer War; it is still following the bloody path: after the Armenian massacres
came the World Wars, the Holocausts of Jewish and
European millions, and the atomic incinerations of
Nagasaki and Hiroshima; then came Korea, Vietnam,
and widespread civil war in Africa, Latin America and,
most recently, Europe, not to mention the brutal
repression of one small country after another by self-
appointed "peacekeeping" superpowers.

If religion has had no impact on the shedding of this
blood (has it done anything other than aid and abet it?)
then why the need for it? How is it that we have become so numbed, that we can pretend our faith is one
of resurrection and life, when in reality it serves as one
of the worst flashpoints of conflict in our culture of
death?

We live in a world of megadeath, on lands reddened
by its original peoples, and saddened with the tears of
unwilling captives. We missionize and maim, westernize
and rob, torture and starve the same fellow humans
around the globe. We kill each other, but not only that;
we abuse the Earth, our common mother.

We kill animals so as to be able to eat the dead. We make of our rivers, lakes, and seas, cesspools of leaden lifelessness. We pillage and burn our forests, then seek to determine why the raped earth beneath them dries into desert. We violate the mountains and line our pocket-books with the sum of their gleaming ore. We poison our air.

Beyond the tide of materialism that encroaches our is-land of survival, the flood of death rises yet higher. We have attempted to mechanize, control, restrict, the very rhythms of the life process itself, and made our women's wombs into tombs. Chilled test tubes are the incubators of our perverted progress.

WHERE IS THE FAITH that truly trusts in Life? Where is the faith that seeks to bring her message to a world sliding down the slope of death? Where is the religion of Life? A religion that sets forth all the living as sacred? A religion that sees the human experience as only one paradigm in the whole connected web of nature?

Is our "God" the god of man alone? Can a Creator-God really bring into being creatures whose sole function is to serve the interests of themselves? Or is such belief really a smokescreen for our narrow schizophrenia, for the un-holy greed that has brought our environment to the brink of destruction on which it now teeters? Put quite another way, do alligators live solely to be skinned for expensive shoes and luggage? Don't they – doesn't every life-form – have an intrinsic right to exist?

It is time to recognize, as do increasing awakened numbers, that the old split-brain approach that perceives man's existence in a vacuum dooms humankind, and species uncounted, to oblivion.

We are in need of a religion of Life that sees the world in more than merely utilitarian terms. A religion that reveres all life as valuable in itself; that sees Earth as an extension of self, and if wounded, as an injury to self.

We need a religion that recognizes the interdependence of man and this world; which sees that the atmosphere surrounding our globe is the same air we breathe, and part and parcel of our lungs – that Earth's water is no different from the saliva in our mouths.

We need a religion that rediscovers the idealism that existed before institutionalism; to rediscover the primordial awe felt by ancient man when he first beheld creation spiraling outside of his insignificant self.

John Africa found such a faith and taught its simple, clear ways to others. In keeping with his natural simplicity, he called that faith Life. "Revere life," he taught: "Protect life, move in harmony with life." Founding the

MOVE Organization on this life-affirming principle, he imbued his followers with an indomitable will to practice them and proclaim them to the world.

He explained to them the worth and power of unity, the relevance and necessity of natural law, and the meaning of resistance and rebellion against a system bent on global self-destruction.

He taught that Earth cannot be a mere way station for the next world, to be fouled, spoiled, or ignored.

CHRISTENDOM

Isn't it odd

that Christendom – that huge body of humankind that claims spiritual descent from the Jewish carpenter of Nazareth – claims to pray to and adore a being who was a prisoner of Roman power, an inmate on the empire's death row? That the one it considers the personification of the Creator of the Universe was tortured, humiliated, beaten, and crucified on a barren scrap of land on the imperial periphery, at Golgotha, the place of the skull? That the majority of its adherents strenuously support the State's execution of thousands of imprisoned citizens? That the overwhelming majority of its judges, prosecutors, and lawyers – those who condemn, prosecute, and sell out the condemned – claim to be followers of the fettered, spat-upon, naked God?

D. Klein

Spirit War

IN AN AGE when the national currency is fear, not
from external threats, but from domestic ones, prisons
have become places of pronounced spiritual and psychic assault. It is not surprising: as an old adage
teaches, "Nothing so concentrates the mind as death."
While the truism has obvious resonance to the thousands on death row, it also has its echoes for thousands more who face "life" terms. Here in morgue-like
holding pens of Pennsylvania's penitentiaries, "life"
literally sentences one to imprisonment for the length
of one's natural lifespan, with no possibility of parole.
"Life" is thus but a grim metaphor for death, for only
death releases one from its shackles. "Life," it might be
said, is merely slow death.

Faced with the spectral imminence of slow death, it is
not unusual that for some, prison becomes a place of
spiritual renewal. Often, it is men who fled religion in
society at large who seek its solace in the secular hell of
society behind bars. Sometimes their searches for spiritual meaning are lauded as evidence of personal progress; sometimes they are discounted as nothing but
jailhouse conversions. Some may be. Others are surely
not. Who can peer into the well of another's spirit?

It is not rare for a prisoner to receive, unsolicited, a religious tract from a group wholly unknown to the recipient. The pamphlet, some four to eight pages, is small – palm-sized – with biblical verses scattered throughout. "Jesus saves!" it may trumpet. Or, "Do you know where you'll be spending eternity?"

Well-intentioned as they are, prison tracts often have the opposite of their desired effect. No matter how eloquently or cleverly they purport to spread good-will and fraternal encouragement, their essence is the same. Though they profess to care deeply about where the objects of their missionary zeal will land after death, few spare a thought for how they may spend the rest of their earthly lives. While their piety is concentrated on the Hereafter, it forgets the Here. Their writers, it seems, are so intoxicated with the thought of heaven, they are content to close an eye to the simmering hell they have helped create on earth.

They endorse, by their silence, the very systems that consign their correspondents to life-long imprisonment and scheduled death.

Often, a tract's content makes it almost impossible for the reader to escape a deeply felt suspicion that those who have sent it to him are fixated wholly on the state of his hereafter – that they couldn't give a damn about his living flesh and living soul.

IS THIS NOT STRANGE, the prisoner muses, given the spiritual adherence they claim to the teachings of a crucified God? Is it not remarkable, coming from believers of a Man-God who gave his life as divine ransom for the souls of sinners? Why is it, he asks himself, that so many Christians want to rush into a grave, those they want to *save?*

Poetry of the Justice of Freedom of spirit beyond we reach beyond Liberation

IMPRISONMENT

JUST BECAUSE your body is in prison doesn't mean your mind isn't free, and even though this thought might be trite, there is some truth in it, because we *are* our minds. In the deepest sense we are our spirits. When you think of a person, or of your own body – is not this a prison in some sense? Are we not in a prison of time? We age, we lose our faculties, but that doesn't mean we cannot overcome, and we do that by the power of mind and spirit. **We reach beyond.**

Christian? Christ-like?

For centuries in America, the term "Christian" has
been virtually synonymous with "white." It was used
not so much to distinguish believers from unbelievers,
but civilized, light-skinned colonists from uncivilized,
dark-skinned natives – the so-called primitive Africans,
savage Indians, and other such heathen. It was a con-
venient spiritual underpinning for the sociopolitical
economic order, that is, the "order" of white supremacy and domination. In such a context, the conversion of a non-white to the dominant, European faith
meant next to nothing, for what did it matter what
faith lived in the heart of a man, if his skin remained
black or red?

Virginia's Act of 1667 was no anomaly. A similar act
became law shortly afterward in South Carolina, and in
another colony, an act passed in 1690 declared quite
openly that "no slave shall be free by becoming a
Christian." And so, new generations of Christians were
baptized, and new generations of preachers, holding
them in the thrall of a system that made reading the

Scriptures for themselves a capital crime, continued
to intone submission: "Slaves, obey your masters."

What did "Christianity" mean to those tens and
hundreds of thousands of men, women, and children
brought to our shores in shackles from the west coast
of Africa? What did it mean to those hardy survivors of
the dreaded Middle Passage who were forced to learn
a new, foreign language and forbidden to speak their
own tongue under threat of the lash? No less important,
what does it mean today, to their great grandchildren,
now legally free to practice the religion of their choice?

Should Afro-Americans praise the god of men who
brought their forebears here in fetid, feverish holds?
A god whose people wiped out all but the last vestiges
of a native population? A god of invaders and
slavemasters? Should anyone?

Formed in the age of Roman imperial supremacy and
Palestinian servitude, Christianity became, in America,
the faith of the slavemaster, the alleged belief of the
rich, the protector of the propertied. For the slave,
though, it was more farce than faith; in his eyes what
was truly worshipped by all was wealth.

Indeed, "Christianity" became cultural shorthand for
the status quo, the existing system of naked, race-based
oppression. The fiction that the Euro-American conquest
of the New World was motivated by efforts to "convert"

indigenous peoples, or that African slavery was necessi-
tated by a desire to bring "the gospel" to the "natives"
is rebuffed by the hand of history. One need only examine the past five centuries from a native perspective –
centuries that brought devastating disease, bloody
persecution, rampant alcoholism, and ultimately, con-
finement in concentration camp-like reservations – to
understand why the god of the pale-faced invaders
seemed less a Great Spirit of goodness than a demon
of destruction.

We have already seen above that even conversion had
no real impact on the convert's state of bondage. As
generations yet unborn were to remark, with a truth
that resonated equally well for one of African descent as
for the native American: "When the Europeans came,
they had their Bible and we had our land; now, they
have our land, and we have their Bible."

Did the native or the slave really expect his master to
sacrifice property and power on the altar of piety? The
story of the Cherokee, derisively referred to as the
"White Indians," reveals a disturbing answer.[1]

In religion, education, cultural and political life, and even
architecture, the Eastern Cherokee adopted European
forms of life to a far greater degree than any other tribe
in North America. By the early 1800s, they were building

---

[1] For documentation of Cherokee history, see John Ehle, *Trail of Tears: The Rise and
Fall of the Cherokee Nation* (New York: Anchor/Doubleday, 1988).

wood and brick homes; they also founded a capital, New Echota, organized a Cherokee Supreme Court, and published a newspaper in an alphabet developed by their famed linguist Sequoyah, a.k.a. George Gist.

Baptist and Moravian churches converted significant numbers to their faiths. The Cherokee were, relatively speaking at least, a wealthy people, with successful crafts and farming operations and hundreds of thousands of head of cattle, horses, and mules. So similar were they to whites that they owned a population of several thousand black slaves. Here was a tribe that was by all measurements a "civilized" tribe: it was Christian, literate, propertied, and law-abiding.

Cherokee "progress" did not come without a cost. Aside from the fact that it meant the destruction and replacement of their own indigenous culture by a European replica, it fueled the resentment of a white economic elite driven by supremacist and expansionist goals. In addition, poorer colonists agitated against their "red" competitors, and the government intervened. Before long, the Cherokee became victims of the same white greed that was to destroy every other native tribe.

Legal victory brought new hopes to the Cherokee in 1832, when they brought suit in the Supreme Court and won a judgment against Georgia, whose "Indian statutes" were declared unconstitutional and thus unenforceable. In *Worcester & Butler v. Georgia* (1832) the Court held:

> The Cherokee Nation then, is a distinct community, occupying its own territory, with boundaries accurately described, in which the laws of Georgia can have no force, and which the citizens of Georgia have no right to enter but with the assent of the Cherokees themselves or in conformity with treaties and the Acts of Congress.

Yet President Andrew "Indian Killer" Jackson refused to follow the ruling and was quoted by journalist Horace Greeley as saying, "[Chief Justice] John Marshall has made his decision; let him enforce it now if he can."

Apparently he couldn't. Already the same year, large tracts of Cherokee ancestral lands were surveyed, divided up, and assigned to white settlers by lottery. By the end of the decade, Georgia's entire Cherokee population was decimated. Evicted from their lands under force of martial "law," whole settlements were marched off to faraway Oklahoma under military escort, straggling along a wintry Trail of Tears whose hardships cost them (and their black slaves, though these were never deemed important enough to count) thousands of lives.

"Civilized" and "Christianized," the Cherokee still lost everything dear to them – their ancestral grounds, their homes and livestock, their children, their women, their elderly, their sick – all because other "Christians" wanted their land. Yet to white minds this unholy program of "resettlement" entailed no losses: it was simply another step in building the foundation on which the very existence of most southern and western states rests.

Today, the Cherokee exist only as a remnant of the past, their reservations an attraction for passing tourists. As for the descendants of Virginia's Christian slaves, they are now free, but the vast majority are still dutifully Christian. True, their churches have remained distinct from white churches in many ways. But those cultural trappings aside, one is tempted to wonder whether the black church doesn't carry the selfsame mission as its white counterpart – and whether the vision that guides it isn't the same.

Certainly there have been men and women in every generation who have raised their voices to rouse their fellow brethren from stultifying slumber. In the fifties and sixties, one of the more notable of these, Dr. Martin

Luther King, Jr., brought a new vitality to a church that up till then had largely sought the solace of martyred silence.

King's church was crippled not only by white supremacist terrorism, however. Equally crippling was its own counsel of quietude. Even in the face of naked injustice, there were clergymen – most white, but some black – who sought to emasculate his message: "Slow down!" "Hush, don't create such a stir!" "Wait for the right time." In a time of unprecedented struggle against the beast of American apartheid, they chose to stand firm in support of the status quo, to sprinkle on the meek and the dissatisfied alike the unholy holy water of centuries.

King's legacy lives on, but it has been twisted. His name and his words have become tools in the hands of the cleverest amongst his enemies to attack, belittle, and deny the very people he sought to serve. His dreams – eloquently set to paper in speeches or essays such as *Letter from a Birmingham Jail* – have been transformed, in the mouths of the powerful, into nightmarish excuses for new chapters of negrophobia, and into attacks on those few, limited, forward steps such as affirmative action, which – if it did nothing else – was at least able to open doors previously sealed by judicial decree.

In our own time, Jean-Bertrand Aristide has noted how Haiti's history has been marked by two imperialisms, political and religious, and how the second has resulted in the development of a theology that serves only to zombify the spirit of the people in order to further subjugate them.

Jesuit scholar Ignacio Martin-Baró has used the Latin-American context – in particular the bitter milieu of countries scarred by recurring civil strife – to similarly illustrate the continuing use of religion as a weapon of psychological warfare against the poor and oppressed.[2] Writing of the dueling purposes of the evangelical church and the Christian base communities in Brazil, he points out that whereas the latter have "gradually assumed a critical tendency" that questions the existing social order, the former has retained a "pentecostal posture of submission, marginalizing its converts and driving them away from any form of protest." He goes on:

> [In] the banana plantation zones of Guapiles, Costa Rica, where aggressive labor unions have traditionally held sway...the "Christians" (as they call themselves) not only do not join political or labor organizations but also oppose the struggles of working people and frequently work as scabs or strikebreakers. These "Christians" have become the banana bosses' trusted workers, and the bosses throw all their support behind the local evangelical churches and pressure their workers to join them.

Writings for a Liberation Theology, 142

---

[2] Fr. Martin-Baró, five fellow priests, and their housekeepers were assassinated in November 1989 by a U.S.-trained and -armed military death squad in El Salvador.

Clearly, no matter how long ago the stone of white religious hypocrisy was cast into the waters of black and native consciousness, we still live in its ever-widening ripples.

At root, the message of the Bible is one of liberation. In the Old Testament it is exemplified by the exodus of the Jewish slaves from Egyptian bondage; in the New, by the coming of a Messiah who (it is promised) will save his people from the yoke of oppression.

Until those who today call themselves "Christians" acknowledge the carnage that has been carried out in his name, it is hard to see how they cannot but continue to commit deeds of devastation and evil. In his name they go on fighting wars of avarice, campaigns of greed, legalized land-theft, and regulated robbery; they go on firing their holy hatreds against the rest of the world. In the very shadow of the cross, they continue to pillage and rape. And in the name of one who, they claim, came "to set captives free," they continue to enslave.

Miracles

*"Woe unto you that are rich,
for ye have received your consolation."*

Not of a god of thunder,
a god of silk,
a god of the rich
did the carpenter speak,
but of a God of compassion,
of peace, of a day brighter
than today;

a God whose miracles still work
in the slave pens and shacks,
in the projects,
in the hellish daily life of the poor
and the oppressed –

not miracles
like walking on waves,
transforming water into wine,
but miracles of love arising
in hearts where it seems least
likely to flourish –

here and there
in the *barrios* and the *favelas*,
among those who have least,
beat hearts of hope,
fly sparks of Overcoming.

The Faith
of Slaves

The tradition of the dead weighs like a nightmare
on the brain of the living.

Karl Marx, *The 18th Brumaire of Louis Bonaparte*

AS IN ANTIQUITY, the black church was born in the
womb of oppression, and its adherents labored under
the heel of slavery. In a climate of general repression,
blacks (even so-called "freed" slaves) were prohibited
from a wide range of jobs and crafts.

One area begrudgingly allowed them was that of
preacher. It was a useful allowance, for an obeisant
minister – especially one who believed in the efficacy of
long-suffering over rebellion – could exercise tremendous influence over his fellow captives and save his
white "Massa" countless difficulties. Vestiges of the
same attitude can be seen in a recent controversy that
surfaced during Christine Todd Whitman's first guberna-
torial campaign in New Jersey: GOP strategists allegedly
donated considerable sums to black preachers, who in
turn promised to urge their congregations to refrain
from voting. (The ministers in question, of course,
vociferously denied all knowledge of this.)

On the positive side, the black pulpit has been a powerful battery that energized the struggle for civil rights,
and as such, other human rights movements in the
late twentieth century. It is noteworthy that the most
influential African-Americans of our time have been
clergymen, albeit of many varied religious traditions.
Dr. Martin Luther King, Jr. and Minister Malcolm X (El
Hajj Malik El-Shabazz) are only two of many who
come to mind.

King's influence has been reflected in the recent past in
many ways, especially in the widened access blacks
have gained to professions and positions previously
closed to them before the passage of various civil rights
laws. The influence of Malcolm X, while equally evident
in the same basic realms, is also reflected in the emer-
gence of a new and different consciousness, particularly in the Black Panther Party and many other similar
black nationalist organizations across America and the
black world in the seventies.

The first, though perceived by many of his contempo-
raries as a radical, was at base a traditionalist whose
views were largely synchronous with the conservativism
of the black church in which he was raised. The second, known in many circles solely for his searing revolutionary oratory, complemented (at least in his later years)
the radicalism of his earlier message with a more conser-
vative spirituality colored by Arabic-influenced Islam.

Both were assassinated in the prime of their lives as
they stood on the brink of exercising unprecedented
influence on national and international affairs.

WHEREAS KING was a dyed-in-the-wool Baptist,
Malcolm X was proudly non-Christian and regarded
Christianity as a white man's religion, wielded by slave
masters to control their black chattel. He excoriated the
kind of Afrophobic religious thinking described in
Blyden's *Islam, Christianity and the Negro* (1888), where
the following observations are recorded:

> It was our lot not long ago to hear an illiterate negro
> in a prayer meeting in New York entreat the deity to
> extend his "lily-white hands" and bless the waiting
> congregation. Another, with no greater amount of
> culture, preaching from John 3:2: "We shall be like
> Him," etc. He exclaimed, "Brethren, imagine a beau-
> tiful white man with blue eyes, rosy cheeks and
> flaxen hair, and we shall be like Him." The concep-
> tions of these worshippers were what they had gath-
> ered from plastic and pictorial representations as well
> as from the characteristics of the dominant race
> around them.

Such psychological enslavement might seem unbeliev-
ably blatant to us today, yet to our black great-grand-
parents it was simply an expression of a lingering
self-hatred that even emancipation could not drown

from the subconscious. Its echoes reverberate even in the present.

One example is the depiction of the deity that continues in black churches: of a white, blue-eyed Christ peering down upon the congregation through shimmering stained-glass windows. It might seem like a small thing in itself, but coupled with the undeniable fact of America's persisting caste system, the power of suggestion it possesses is tremendous. Perhaps it is such images that have disenchanted and alienated many African-Americans and turned them from the churches of their youth to the various schools of Islam, to pre-American or syncretic African faiths, or to the rejection of the religious dimension of life *in toto.*

WHEN THE CHILDREN OF ISRAEL were delivered from Egyptian bondage, they traversed the desert for over forty years, until almost all those who had lived in slavery had passed away. One reading of that wilderness experience regards it as a necessary prerequisite to what was to follow: it concludes that no one with a slave psychology could live as a truly free person in the Promised Land and that, moreover, a survivor's psyche would be so indelibly etched with the taint of enslavement that it would even pose a danger to the next generation.

We who are familiar with the biblical account of the same exodus recall that, in times of peril, hunger, and doubt, a cry arose from the people, longing for the land of their oppression:

> And when Pharaoh drew nigh, the children of Israel lifted up their eyes, and behold, the Egyptians marched after them; and they were sore afraid; and the children of Israel cried out unto the Lord.

> And they said unto Moses, because there were no graves in Egypt, hast thou taken us away to die in the wilderness? Wherefore hast thou dealt thus with us, to carry us forth out of Egypt? *(Ex. 14:10–11)*

The Jews later mimicked their Egyptian masters by fashioning an idol in the form of a molten golden calf – an ancient example of a people adopting the religious mores of their oppressors.

In our own era and culture, the Reverend Albert Cleage created considerable controversy in Detroit when he commissioned a stained-glass montage and altarpiece for his Shrine of the Black Madonna, which featured an African Mary with an African Christ.

Not unlike the Israelites before them, it has taken generations for a once-enslaved people to reach the point of mental freedom from which they can see the face of the divine in themselves.

When the face and the presence of the divine can be glimpsed in the smile of a child – or the hope of a bride, the fecundity of a green field, the wisdom of the ancients – it is a small sign that a people are emerging from the dark coffin of bondage.

Hope

Jennifer Beach

What keeps me alive?

My belief – my religion, which I call Life – the teachings of John Africa and the example of my MOVE brothers and sisters across the state, many of whom have survived imprisonment for years and years. Their example has buoyed me up over fourteen years behind bars. Also, my faith in the power of commitment, in the power of family, in the power of love, of community, of God. I could give you one term instead of four or five. "Family," for example, means unity, commitment, love. That is "family." The other thing, of course, is laughter. Very simply, it's human to laugh and to find humor, even in something small. Every day. Every day there is *something* to laugh about! That keeps me human.

Fritz Eichenberg

SALT
OF THE
EARTH

Blessed are they
who are persecuted
for righteousness' sake;
for theirs is
the kingdom of heaven.

Blessed are ye,
when men revile you
and persecute you,
and say all manner of evil
against you falsely,
for my sake.

Rejoice,
and be exceeding glad,
for great is your reward in heaven:
for so persecuted they
the prophets before you.

Ye are the salt of the earth;
and if salt loses its savor,
of what use is it?
It is good for nothing
but to be cast out
and trodden underfoot.

Jesus of Nazareth (Mt. 5:10 –13)

IT DOES NOT TAKE a biblical scholar to see that the righteous have indeed been persecuted throughout history. The "meek" may well one day "inherit the earth," yet for the last few millennia it has been the exclusive property of those in power, whilst the meek have inherited the grave.

American history provides plenty to illustrate the point: as an unsurpassed disinheritor of aboriginal peoples, it is an imperialistic nation-state composed primarily of stolen or forcibly seized territories. Were the so-called founding fathers meek, that they should inherit this piece of earth?

Central to the question is the proposition that America is a Christian nation – a nation composed of men and women eager to be persecuted for righteousness' sake. If this be so, then it is Christian to wipe out whole native peoples and commend their ravaged remnants to barren reservations; it is Christian to steal millions of people from their overseas homelands and hold them in bondage for centuries; it is Christian to cast thousands of Japanese into concentration camps and to seize their properties on the pretext of that magical word "security." If it is really so, then it is Christian to vaporize hundreds of thousands of fellow humans by dropping an atomic bomb on them, as a global "demonstration" of power; Christian to cage millions and execute thousands; Christian to devise a socio-economic system that marginalizes the weak, the awkward, the inarticulate, the downtrodden poor. Or are we to conclude that perhaps America is not a Christian nation after all?

For those faceless, nameless black, brown, and yellow millions who have been savaged by America, it might even appear that the course of its history has been guided by some demonic orientation. Instead of Christ, perhaps Dracula should be substituted for this nation's guiding god – for has it not sucked the blood of the planet's other peoples for two centuries? Does it not do so now?

Where is the God of the poor, the powerless, the damned, the crushed? Where, in national political life, is even one voice of Christ-like compassion heard?

The Roman historian Tacitus described the first Christians as a "sect" who entered his city "clad in filthy gabardines" and "smelling of garlic," a people of poverty, the salt of the earth. How, we must ask, did they come from that to this: from a tribe of the lowly to the vampires of the planet?

In order to trace the devolution, we must begin by admitting that a second crucifixion of Christ has taken place, not by a second Roman empire, but by the very men and women who bear his name: his Church.

Revolution is not a *word* but an *application*; it is not *war* but *peace*; it does not *weaken*, but *strengthens*. Revolution does not cause *separation*; it generates *togetherness*.

John Africa, *Strategic Revolution*

Never doubt that a small group of committed people can change the world; indeed, it's the only thing that ever has.   Margaret Mead

FOR MILLIONS, perhaps billions of us, life is a search, a journey of seeking for that which we found unfulfilled in our youth. We search for love; we search for family; we search for community. And in so doing, we seek the completion of Self in others, in the larger Self where similar selves are united in commonality – in community.

As we search and grow, we find that modern life, with its bursting balloons of materialism, leaves us more and more empty inside; "things" that once seemed to fill us now fail to bridge the gaping chasms in our psyche. Our inner selves are pulled in too many ways at once – the demands of work here, and social obligations there, the pressures of financial need (or the lesser burdens of wealth), public respon-

sibilities, the needs and wants of our private sphere –
and finally they break, atomized, meaningless.

The dominant societal ideology of the hour is a perverse
individuality hammered into our consciousness by myth
and legend. It ignores the historical verity of community – of groups striving to move the social order forward. It ignores the reality that people working together
are the only viable solution to any social problem.

As human beings, we are at root social creatures. Outside the bonds of our familial and social relations, we
cannot truly live. Our very sanity depends on them. We
are birthed in and into community. We grow in community. Community determines who we are. It is not the
individual self *per se,* but its place in the broader social
network of human society that defines our identity and
gives our life meaning.

Whether in religious, political, economic, or educational
matters, collectivity is a basic requisite for meaning. Can
there truly be a religion of one? What political action
can be effectively undertaken by a lone person? Doesn't
every step toward economic progress require at least
some level of social agreement – some willingness to put
aside antagonisms – for it to function? Doesn't education, especially as it is presently constituted, consist
largely of teaching youth how to play by the rules of the
broader social order? Is it purely coincidental that stu-

dents are organized into "classes"? Doesn't it teach
them how to acquiesce, not how – or even whether –
to transform the status quo?

And what of a circumstance in which the status quo is
unfair or oppressive? Such can be said to have given rise
to a community of resistance, known as the MOVE Organization, which, in the words of its legendary founder
John Africa, has as its *raison d'être* total liberation:

> The MOVE organization is a powerful family of revo-
> lutionaries, fixed in principle, strong in cohesion,
> steady as the foundation of a massive tree. A people
> totally equipped with the profound understanding of
> simple assertion, collective commitment, unbending
> direction.
>
> While the so-called educators talk of love, mouth the
> necessity for peace, we live peace, assert the power
> of love, comprehend the urgency of freedom. The
> reformed world system cannot teach love while mak-
> ing allowances for hate, peace while making allow-
> ances for war, freedom while making allowances for
> the inconsistent shackles of enslavement. For to make
> allowances for sickness is to be unhealthy; to make
> concessions with slavery is to be enslaved; to compro-
> mise with the person of compromise is to be as the
> person you are compromising with.[1]

---

[1] "On the Move: from the Writings of John Africa," *Philadelphia Tribune*, 28 June
1975, 17.

John Africa founded and forged a remarkable family, a small but potent community of resistance that took Life as its creed and fought to protect the lives of all the living, even animals like dogs and cats.

Everyone is born into the family of their flesh; here was one of choice, commitment, and faith. It was a family embattled, but a family nonetheless. It lives, grows, and thrives today. Long live John Africa's revolutionary family!

Men of the Cloth

Pam Africa, minister and disciple of the teaching of John Africa, tells the true tale of a meeting between the latter and a man of the cloth behind the old headquarters of the MOVE Organization in the Powelton Village section of West Philadelphia.

The scene: a man, middle-aged, bearded, booted and blue-jeaned, is called to the back door by the leader of a small group from a nearby church. Though both are black, they present a fascinating tableau of difference. The one wears a T-shirt, sweat soaking his breast; the other is impeccably dressed in silk suit and tie, the only touch missing is coattails. The one's hair is rough, gray-fringed, uncombed, and hanging like ropes to his shoulders; the other's is pomaded, greased and brushed smooth – the head of a preacher-man.

The air is thick and charged with controversy, for the city is threatening to remove MOVE from their property and the neighborhood after a series of highly publicized confrontations with the police that has left several MOVE men and women beaten and bloody, and one MOVE baby dead.

"So, you're sayin', all I gotta do is pray, and everything
will be all right?"

"That's what I'm saying, brotha."

"If I pray, the cops will stop beatin' up my people?"

"Yes! That's what I'm saying, brotha."

"If I pray the cops will stop killin' us?"

"Yes! Pray – in Jesus name, brother – 'cause the Bible
say, 'Ask, and it shall be given unto you.' That's it,
brother."

"And if I pray, our people will truly be free?"

"Uh-huh. Yessir, brother!"

"Well, c'mon, Reverend. Let's pray then."

John Africa drops to his knees, oblivious of the soft
mud already staining his jeans.

"Whoa! Whatcha doin', brotha?"

"You said we needa pray, right?"

"Uhh…uhh…"

"Come on, Rev, pray with me, okay?"

"I…I…I meant, pray in the church."

"Why, Reverend? Ain't God out here in the open air,
ain't God all around us? Come on! Let's kneel down
here on God's earth and pray."

At this point the Reverend backs up, and John Africa
says, "What's the matter? I thought you said we should
pray. Well, come on down here and pray with me."

The Reverend continues to stand there, staring. John

Africa asks again, "What's the matter, man? That suit
you got on more important than God? I thought you
said you believed in God. This dirt *is* God, so why don't
you kneel down here and pray with me?"
"Well, uh…excuse me, brotha, but I gotta be getting
back to my church."

At this point the people standing around the two men
begin to speak: "You see that? That man is down there
on his *knees* in the dirt; he *got* to be for real. That
Reverend ain't nothin' but a phoney. He scared he
gonna dirty his suit. He talkin' 'bout how he believe in
God. He don't believe in nothin' but that suit."

One woman comments to another, "That preacher's a
hypocrite. See, that's why I don't go to church, cuz I
don't believe in them preachers, cuz they ain't nothin'
but liars; they ain't for real That man there kneelin' in
the dirt *is* for real."

John Africa goes on, "You don't wanna pray with me,
then, Rev?"
"I gotta go, man, uhh…I'm sorry."
"Why you leavin', Rev?"

The dashing preacher beats a hasty retreat from the
muddy yard, more intent, it seems, on saving silk than
souls…

Several years later, and several miles westward, the city

would torch MOVE's home and headquarters with a
helicopter-borne firebomb, incinerating John Africa
and ten other "longhairs" (some of them women and
children) in a massacre plotted to take place on Mother's
Day.

The scene: smoldering remains of an entire neighborhood, only hours before the site of a blistering, billowing
inferno. Philadelphia's men of the cloth have gathered
once again, though only to examine the carnage – not
to weep for the fallen, nor to pray for the dead.

They have come bedecked in robes and collars, the pur-
pose of their gathering to pray in support of the mayor of
a city that has bombed its own citizens, and obliterated,
incinerated, and dismembered its own babies.

The police commissioner, the fire chief, the mayor, and
his officers are almost to a man "Christian" – Baptists or
Catholics, most of them – religious people. Yet these men
who have gathered to pray are not only churchgoers.
They are ministers, pastors, priests! Aside from praying,
though, it seems that they mean to do little. Why should
they? They've just winked at a full-scale war waged over
mere misdemeanors: at the deaths of eleven people
blasted by a sky-bomb, the destruction of dozens of
homes, and the permanent scarring of a neighborhood.

And so they pray and leave for home, their duties ful-
filled. Men of the cloth, yes. But men of the spirit?

Hate's Unkind Counsel

A COOL AUTUMN WIND blew through the chain-link fence and razor-wire cages. Rog, a brilliant jailhouse lawyer, and I were running around in leftist circles warming up for a few games of cage handball. We had scarcely hit twenty laps when a mustached man in a sweater appeared. My counselor. We threw some words at each other, but I kept running. My jogging back faced him, moving away step by step.

"Jamal! Anything you wanna talk about? No rap, huh?"

He walked away, scribbling *pro forma* notes on his clipboard. Rog stopped running.

"What's up, man?"
"Did you see that shit, man?"
"What? Whatchu talking 'bout, Rog?"
"How that dude was lookin' atcha!"
"Whatchu mean, man?"
"Jeezus H. Kee-rist! Didn't ya see how your counselor was lookin' atchu? Talkin' to ya, Mu?"
"Hey, look, man. I don't pay that guy no mind, man."
"That's your *counselor!*"
"That's his title, but what can he do? Can he help me even get a phone call?"

"No, but – "

"See?"

"But that's not the point."

"What *is* the point, then?"

"How that dude was lookin' at you!"

"Whachu sayin', Rog?"

"That dude hates your guts, Jamal!"

"And – ?"

"I jus' never saw a counselor treat a man like that.
How's it make you feel?"

"To be honest, Rog, I never really thought about it. It's
jus' normal, I guess."

"Normal? *My* counselor don't talk to *me* like that! I
looked at that dude's face, and it made my skin crawl,
Mu!"

"Really?"

"No shit, man."

I flashed in memory at his visage, and saw – *really*
saw – what upset Roger so. Here was a face of
naked hatred. Why hadn't I seen it before? How
had I ignored it?

Roger, a man with three first-degree murder convic-
tions, three death sentences and ages beyond of time,
was no Pollyanna. How could he be so profoundly
shocked at what I couldn't even see without his help?

It dawned on me then that I *had* seen my counselor's

tight mask of hatred before, when he wore his gray
guard's uniform, wooden club gripped in a tight white
fist, a leather thong stretched across its back.

Now that he was a counselor, his uniform had changed,
but his face hadn't.

I remembered him escorting naked men to the shower,
weapon in hand.

To me, he was hardly a man from whom one sought
counsel, for his weapon had merely been transformed
into an ink pen and a clipboard; he was an agent, albeit
with another function, of the same State that fought to
steal my life. And even if I had not recognized his hatred
at first, I knew intuitively that there was a profound
distinction between the way he saw Rog, and saw
me – one I couldn't allow myself to see, but which a
white death row prisoner couldn't ignore. Both of us
were sentenced to death (one of us thrice!), yet one of
us he treated as a man; the other as a non-human
beast.

Perhaps I had subconsciously chosen to ignore the distinction before; chosen *not* to see what there was to see
every day: a psychic spittle of hatred, fear, and alienation
splashed against my inner person. More than choice,
though, my willed blindness, pretended invisibility, and
psychological self-distortion were mechanisms of self-
defense: a survival stratagem in a House of Death.

Human Beings

NINETY-FIVE PERCENT of the guards I've met are doing their job simply because they need the money. Like cops and sheriffs, they are men, human beings, and their central concerns, needs, and fears are the same as anyone else's – they need money to pay rent, put bread on the table, provide an education for their children. But they have become part of the system because of their fear; they have bought into it because it is built on fear. Remember, the *system* is not a true reality, but an idea which can be fought and dismantled. People forget that we don't need the system, or the accessories we mistakenly assume are essential for living. We need only the things God gave us: love, family, nature. We must transform the system. That's the challenge. It's do-able, but only if we ourselves do it.

The Spider

NORMAN CALLED OVER, his voice heavy and strangely conspiratorial. "Hey, Mu. Ya bizzy, man?"

"Naw, Norm. I wuz jus doin' a little readin.' But wussup, man?"

"I been lookin' at this mama spider in my cell. She beautiful, man!"

"Yeah?"

"She tiny, but she so strong, man!"

"Uh huh…"

"An' ya know what's amazin'?"

"Whut's dat, Norm?"

"Think 'bout how she make her own home – her web – out of her own body!"

"That's amazin', man."

And indeed it *was* amazing, especially to Norman, a man encaged in utter isolation. Here he sat – would sit for the remainder of his days – in the antiseptic stillness of a supermaximum-security prison block, yet he was not entirely alone. With a quiet, unwitting bravado that defied the State's most stringent efforts to quarantine him, spiders had moved in and built webs in the dark corner under his sink. Now they shared his cell, and he spent hours watching them spin their miraculous silken thread.

Norman watched them give birth. He watched them stalk those few rare flies who entered his cell, only to be trapped. He watched them suck the life sap from their prey until nothing remained but dry husks. He watched them in a deep and reverent wonder, and his cell became a study.

Norman watched, and whenever something truly remarkable occurred, he quietly tapped on the wall. He'd begin in a deep stage-whisper: "Mu – Yo, Mu! Ya bizzy, man?"

I was rarely too busy to listen for fifteen or twenty minutes, and it wasn't long before I found myself sharing his fascination and enthusiasm. And in time, lo and behold, a web scaffold appeared in my own sink-corner.

IN ANCIENT AFRICAN and West Indian folklore, the mother spider – Anansi – looms large. She is a wise and protective being who knows proverbs and possesses the gift of prophecy.

A famous Ghanian tale tells of a fire raging in a forest. As the beasts scamper for safety, an antelope feels a tickling sensation. A small dark spider has alighted on her ear. Before she can toss her head to flick it off, however, the spider whispers, "It is I, Anansi. Take me with you – I will repay you." The antelope, more concerned with its own survival than the minor inconvenience of a spider, agrees and runs on to safety, her path directed by Anansi.

Once she reaches safety, Anansi climbs off, thanking the antelope and promising her she won't be forgotten. Several seasons later, the antelope finds herself and her offspring threatened again, this time by hunters. Her little one is too young to run, so she instructs it to drop to the ground and hide itself in the shrubbery. Then, leaping from the undergrowth, she distracts the hunters and leads them away from her baby. Arrows whiz through the air, but the antelope is too swift. Finally the hunters give up the chase and leave the forest.

Cautiously, she returns to find her young one, whose faint cry she hears but cannot place. Where is her baby? Try as she might, she can't find her.

Just then, Anansi lets herself down from a tree limb on her slim silken cord, and announces her presence. Whispering to the mother antelope, she directs her to a clump of shrubs where, hidden under a tightly-woven protective net, lies her baby. "I told you I wouldn't forget you," Anansi reminds her.

FOR NORMAN, the target of a hunt no less deadly than that of an antelope in the jungle, Anansi was vital company. In a cell constructed to maximize human loneliness – a site designed to kill the mind – Anansi was a source of friendship and wonder. In a concrete tomb erected to smother men to death, she was a tiny, marvelous reflection of life. She brightened a man's day, and made it meaningful. Nature amid the unnatural.

The Fall

Each year, when summer fades and the air cools, a sense of sadness pervades. Leaf-life readies its swan dive of separation from mother tree in an explosion of color; flowers shrivel, and the sound of insect life dies away; even sweet birdsong pales.

The earth, like an old woman, prepares for death. She covers herself often with snow, and sunfire leaves her face. Her hair, once green and lush, thins and falls; her blood, her blue pulsing blood, slows to a trickle and eventually freezes still. All the markers of death gather around her like a storm.

Who can but grieve? Only the certainty of renewal mitigates the pervasive sense of loss: the knowledge that behind the cold night lies the spring morn; that beneath fallowed earth lies a mighty heart athrob with life; that life lives within life, and goes forever on.

Children

IN JONATHAN KOZOL'S BOOK *Amazing Grace,*
he demonstrates something of very positive significance:
the power of a child's hope. The children whose stories
he tells live in the worst possible conditions in the
world – in drug-ridden slums – yet they still have an
innate hope.

There is of course, a negative part to it that remains despite this hope, and that is the reality of the world around
them. The children have hope, but they are not blind to
the fact that they are often ignored, and sometimes even
scorned, by the social order.

There's a little boy, David, in the book, who tells Kozol
that he saw the mayor of New York City on TV, and he
says, "I don't like him." Kozol asks, "Why do you say
that?" And David says, "Because when I look in his eyes,
all I see is coldness. He doesn't understand how poor
people have to live." That is the way that most politicians
in the system, actually most wealthy people, look at poor
children. And the children see this; they sense this coldness coming from the people who literally control their
circumstances – the conditions of the neighborhood, the
state of their education.

Still, many of these children don't give up. Perhaps the best thing we can do for them is to nurture their hope – give them reason for new hopes, and feed the hope already within them so it can grow into something strong that will sustain them through life. Elie Wiesel says that the greatest evil in the world is not anger or hatred, but indifference. If that is true, then the opposite is also true: that the greatest love we can show our children is the attention we pay them, the time we take for them. Maybe we serve children best simply by noticing them.

Children do not only have an innate hope; they *are* hope. And more than that: they are our future. As Kahlil Gibran writes, they are like "living arrows sent forth" into infinity, and their souls "dwell in the house of to-morrow…" They carry their hope with them to a future we can't see.

Children come to us fresh from the divine source, from what I call "Mama," from life itself, and they lead us to the same: to the God-force within creation. That is why none of us – no matter our race, creed, religion, or politics – can look at a child and not feel joy. We look at them, and something thrills us to the depth of our hearts. They are living miracles, and when we see them we know that there is a God, that life itself is a miracle. Children show us, with their innocence and clarity, the very face of God in human form.

People have different names for God, and we can't be offended by that. We have to try and understand what they mean. You call him God. I call him Mama. I see God like you see your Mama. The closest relationship there is on earth is the relationship between child and mother. Mama feeds us. Her sun warms us, and her earth gives us food; she provides air, water, pretty flowers in the fields, trees, forests, little birds – she is Life. Life gives life to everything in creation. That, for me, is God. Anyone who studies religion to any depth will find that there is a great cultural and traditional breadth in how people perceive the divine personality. Much of it is colored by social mores, some of it even by politics. People are different. But remember, all the thousands of different names we use for the Creator are man-made, and the Creator is One.

Father Hunger

IT HAS BEEN OVER THREE DECADES since I have looked into his face, but I find him now, sometimes hidden, in the glimpse of a mirror. He was short of stature, shorter than I at ten years, fully, smoothly bald, with a face the color of walnuts. He walked with a slight limp, and smoked cigars, usually Phillies. Although short, he wasn't slight, but powerfully built with a thick, though not fat, form. His voice was deep, with the accents of the South wrapped around each word, sweet and sticky like molasses.

Often his words tickled his sons, and they tossed them among themselves like prizes found in the depths of a Crackerjack box, words wondrous in their newness, their rarity, their difference from all others.

"Boys! Cut out that tusslin', heah me?" And the boys would stop their rasslin', their bellies near bursting with swallowed, swollen laughter, the word vibrating *sotto voce* in their throats: "Tusslin' – tusslin' – tusslin' – tusslin! Tusslin'!" For days – for weeks – these silly little boys had a new toy and, with this one word, reduced each other to teary-eyed fits of fall-on-the-floor laughter. "Tusslin'!"

He was a relatively old man when he seeded these sons, over fifty, and because of his age, he was openly affectionate in a way unusual for a man of his time. He kissed them, dressed them, and taught them, by

Thomas Filmyer/WCB

example, that he loved them. He talked with them. And walked and walked and walked with them.

"Daaad! I wanna riiide!,"
I whined.

"It ain't good for you to ride so much, boy. Walkin' is good for ya. It's good exercise for ya."

Decades later, I would hear that same whine from one of my sons, and my reply would echo my father's.

His eyes were the eyes of age, so discolored by time they seemed blueish, but there was a perpetual twinkle of joy in them, of love and living. He lived just over a decade into this son's life, and his untimely death from illness left holes in the soul.

Without a father, I sought and found father-figures like Black Panther Captain Reggie Schell, Party Defense Minister Huey P. Newton, and indeed, the Party itself, which, in a period of utter void, taught me, fed me, and made me part of a vast and militant family of revolutionaries. Many good men and women became my teachers, my mentors, and my examples of a revo-lutionary ideal – Zayd Malik Shakur, murdered by police when Assata was wounded and taken, and Geronimo ji jaga (a.k.a. Pratt) who commanded the Party's L.A. chap-ter with distinction and defended it from deadly state attacks until his imprisonment as a victim of frame-up and judicial repression – Geronimo, torn from his family and children and separated from them for a quarter of a century.

Here in death row, in the confined sub-stratum of a society where every father is childless, and every man fatherless, those of us who have known the bond of father-son love may at least re-live it in our minds, per-haps even draw strength from it. Those who have not – the unloved – find it virtually impossible to love. They live alienated from everyone around them, at war even with their own families.

Here in this manmade hell, there are countless young men bubbling with bitter hatreds and roiling resentments against their absent fathers. Several have taken to the odd habit of calling me "Papa," an endearment whose irony escapes them.

It has never escaped me. I realize that I live amidst a generation of young men drunk not only with general loneliness, but with the particular, gnawing anguish of father-hunger. I had my own father; later I had the Party, and Geronimo; Delbert, Chuck, Mike, Ed, and Phil; Sundiata, Mutulu, and other oldheads like myself. Who have they had?

Yet for a long time I resisted the nickname. I resented being "Papa" to young men I didn't know, while being denied – by decree of state banishment – the opportunity to be a father to the children of my own flesh and heart. My sons were babies when I was cast into this hell, and no number of letters, cards, or phone calls can ever heal the wounds that they and their sisters have suffered over the long, lonely years of separation.

I was also in denial. For who was the oldhead they were calling? Certainly not me? It took a trip, a trek to the shiny, burnished steel mirror on the wall, where I found my father's face staring back at me, to recognize reality. I am he…and they are me.

Mother-loss

RELATIVELY TALL, mountainous cheekbones, dimples like doughnuts, and skin the color of Indian corn, she left life in the South for what was then the promised land, "up Nawth." Although she lived, loved, raised a family, and worked over half her life "up Nawth," the soft, lyrical accents of her southern tongue never really left her. Words of a single syllable found a new one in her mouth, often rising on the second syllable: "Keith" became "Key-eath," "child" became "Chy'ile," and her reedy, lengthy laughter lit up the room like a holiday. She, and her children, lived in the "peejays" (the projects), but it wasn't until years later (when we were grown) that we understood we had lived in poverty, for our mother made sure our needs were met. She was a gentle woman who spoke well, if at all, of most folk, but she was like a lioness when one of her children was attacked.

In the early '60s, when her daughter got caught up in a neighborhood fracas that boiled out of control, she snapped a broomstick in two, whipped open a path down the block to where her daughter stood paralyzed by terror, grabbed her, and whipped

her way back home. Only when she was safely back indoors did she realize that she had been slashed while outdoors – she never noticed, so powerful was her love for her daughter. Deep rivers of loving strength flowed through her.

A mother's love is the foundation of every love: it is the primary relationship of all human love, the first love we experience and, as such, a profound influence on all subsequent and secondary relationships in life. It is a love that surpasses all reason.

Perhaps that's why I thought she would live forever – that this woman who carried me, my brothers, and my sister, would never know death. For thirty years she smoked Pall Malls and Marlboros, yet still I thought she would live forever. When she died, of emphysema, while I was imprisoned, it was like a lightning bolt to the soul. Never during my entire existence had there been a time when she was not there. Suddenly, on a cold day in February, her breath had ended, and her sweet presence, her wise counsel, was gone forever.

To know one's mother dead, yet remain imprisoned! To imagine her lifeless form while held in shackles! To crush the hope of ever again embracing she who birthed me!

Meeting with a Killer

In Philadelphia, Hank Fahy's name is mud.

Convicted of the 1981 rape-slaying of a girl-child and subsequently sentenced to death, Fahy has dwelt in a virtual netherworld beneath the "usual" hell that is death row. Marked as a baby-rapist, he has had to withstand the loathing and contempt of the many who regard his crime as an act beneath contempt.

Fahy's odyssey into the underworld has not been an easy one: bouts of suicide attempts have alternated with periods of an almost manic evangelical fervor, a living pendulum swinging between visions of hell and heaven, both just beyond his grasp.

In late June, 1995, while under his second death warrant, and with a date to die in July, Hank would come face-to-face with the living personifications of his demons and his angel.

Even while under an active death warrant, with a date to die within two weeks, Fahy was transferred to a Philadelphia city prison (rather than the state prison at Graterford, as is customary).

When he arrived, he was placed in a cell, where the words "Jamie Fahy – Rest in Peace" were scrawled across the wall: Jamie Fahy, a beautiful, troubled, love-starved young girl – beaten, murdered, and allegedly raped – Hank's eighteen-year-old daughter, who was barely four when he entered Hell.

There is more.

From impish whisperings of those around him, he learned an astonishing thing – that the man charged with beating, killing, and raping his daughter was there – not merely in the same prison – but there – on that very block!

As if inevitable, Hank met Mark (not his real name), and the hatred kindled over months melted into rare compassion.

"I hated him, Jamal," Fahy confided, "but when I saw this kid, eighteen years old, I realized what a hell he was in for; and also, I thought about the pain I would be causing his mother if I took something and stuck him."

In every prison in America, murder is no mystery. There are men on death row across the nation awaiting execution for killings committed in prison.

Hank had two weeks of life left. What did he have to lose?

"You know, Jamal, I looked at this eighteen-year-old kid, and I remembered the look on my mother's face when she was alive, when she came to visit me; the shame of

seeing her son on death row; and I didn't have the heart
to tell this kid, but I could see his mother lookin' at him
the same way, and it hurt me, Jamal, it really did, man."

"What hurt you, Hank? Whatchu mean?"

"Well, it was two things. First, this was a set-up; I was
'sposed to kill this kid! Why else would they put us on
the same block? Come on, man. Second, the same
people that put me on death row are gonna put this
kid on death row, but he don't know it yet."

"What did you tell Mark, man?"

"I told him 'I forgive ya, man', and I told him to let his
lawyer know this, and anything I can do to help him and
to keep him off death row, I'll do."

"How did you feel tellin' that boy that, Hank?"

"Ya know, Jamal, I felt good. I felt like the better man,
'cause the same system that plans to kill me, that plans
to kill him, that same system that set us *both* up (for me
to kill him and for him to get killed), can't do what I
did – forgive."

"I loved Jamie, Jamal. She was my heart. But me killin'
that kid can't bring my daughter back, and ya know
what else, Jamal?"

"What's dat, Hank?"

"I wouldn't wish this – death row – on my *worstest*
enemy."

Dialogue

N. Ascencios

IN OUR COUNTRY alone there are over a million men and women – not even counting juveniles – in prisons. There are an estimated three million homeless people. Poverty is widespread, and fear is the national currency. People seek the security of love, yet at the same time they are isolated, alienated – even from themselves. Isolation and alienation are barriers, forces of division. What shatters these barriers is dialogue.

Even in a free democracy, the State always attempts to control dialogue – to decide for its own interests the limits of allowable discourse. In order to be heard, one must have wealth, power, influence, rank. It's the same with the media. The media always quotes the same roundtable of "experts." Where are the voices of the poor, the excluded, the powerless? Absent those voices, absent a recognition of their worth, there can be no true dialogue, and thus no true democracy.

Objectivity
and the Media

OBJECTIVITY IN JOURNALISM is an illusion, a hollow word, yet it becomes so real to its perpetrators, who have been poisoned with the lie from the first day of journalism school, that they end up not only believing in it, but letting it form the whole foundation of their profession. It's always been a great ideal, but in reality it's a misguided belief. And they end up using it to justify everything they do.

When you look at the news today – I'm talking now about national network newscasts – it is astounding that what used to make the local news, if that, is now considered as having national importance. Local crime stories, especially the most lurid ones, become national news stories not because of anything extraordinary about them, but because that is the stuff that sells. It's the old jingle: "If it bleeds, it leads." They don't feed the public pieces that stimulate intelligent thought, pieces that might make people talk or even ask questions about the fundamental relationships of power, rank, and status in this country. They're more interested in sensation.

It's almost as if the average newscast has been reduced and molded to fit Hard Copy or some other such show like that. The end product is trash, but it is trash that has been carefully designed to attract you emotionally, to touch you sensationally, to get you looking (but not thinking). It doesn't provoke you or encourage you to question the fundamentals. The real issues behind a story are often ignored. They're not considered important enough to be raised. That's why many people – not only MOVE, but other groups who are misunderstood and misrepresented – share MOVE's "f.t.p." attitude toward the media: Fuck the press!

By the seventies, people began to admit that the media was in the hip-pocket of big business. Well, today the media *is* big business. The major media organizations are not just controlled by it – they are part of it. Many of them are owned by huge multinational corporations. And if you think they don't control what comes over the air, you're in for a surprise. If I control your paycheck, I tell you what to say and what not to say.

When Rizzo was mayor, he was always taking the Philadelphia media to task and – especially during the time of the 1978 MOVE confrontation – accusing them of stirring things up with their advocacy journalism. They lacked objectivity, he complained. Well, Rizzo was right on one

Frances Jetter

count, because, as I said earlier, journalistic "objectivity" is non-existent. Who's objective? But as far as the slant of their advocacy goes, I don't know who Rizzo thinks they were advocating. It sure wasn't MOVE.

Neither the brutal police assault on the MOVE compound in August 1978 nor the bombing of their new compound in May 1985 – in which eleven of their members were killed, and a whole neighborhood was destroyed – could ever have happened without the media. It was in their interest to create the fires of carnage and hatred, and feed those fires. The media built the scaffolding around the MOVE standoff, and the information they disseminated became the catalyst for the final conflagration. The next step after that was for them to whitewash the whole thing to save face for the "investigative" commission.

The frightening thing is that the press's involvement in the MOVE debacle was in no way unique; it is instructive for the present, the future, and for any number of contexts and loci, not just racist Philadelphia. Don't forget – two things always define the media's perspective: money and power. And the resulting "blindness" is therefore often willful.

I remember being down in Philadelphia at my petition hearing in the fall of 1995 – I was being shuttled back to the prison, and the sheriff had turned the radio on. The newscaster was announcing that ABC had just been acquired by the Disney Corporation. I laughed. I was in the back of the van laughing and laughing and thinking to myself that it won't be long before they have Mickey Mouse and Donald Duck on the evening news.

On a deeper level, of course, it's no laughing matter. When the power of the press is exercised in concert with the political machinery that is in place today – I'm talking about the right wing shift in American politics – what you have is a dangerous, malevolent concoction. It might sound paranoid, but that's what you have.

Just recently there's been considerable controversy about the planes that were shot down over Cuba. The alternative press is asking some interesting questions, but what about the mainstream media? There's a whole history to this incident that is being withheld by the government and the press. I can't help wondering about the fact that when Cuba was the whorehouse of the Caribbean – when it was a Mafia safe-haven – you didn't hear anybody talking about invading Cuba or changing the government. It was only when a government of the Cubans' own choice rose to power and said that they were no longer willing to be our whorehouse – "We are an independent sovereign country, and we will have the government we want, not the government you want" – that our government began plotting to kill President Castro and to destroy Cuba through an economic blockade that, according to international law, amounted to an act of war. Has our government, our press, acted on the right side of history? Have they stood on the right side of fundamental justice?

Cuba's only one of many examples. Fundamentally, the United States Government has allied itself for decades with some of the darkest forces in history for the sake of economic gain, for political self-interest, for the protection of the status quo. And it continues to do so, domestically as well. That's why we have the likes of David Duke running for governor and the likes of Pat Buchanan running for President (in spite of having Klansmen on his staff). It's why everybody is talking about welfare queens and slamming the poor. It is also why the safest political platform of the decade is based on promises of "getting tough on crime." Their line is that it's okay to despise the poor, because they have it "too good" anyway. Besides, they claim, it's the poor, the minorities who are causing a rise in violent crime: "What we need is more executions. What we need to do is start chopping people's heads off…" The level of political discourse in our country is anti-life. And the press is not innocent.

Violence

Violence violates the self.

Yet that's exactly what the system believes in, what the system preaches, what the system practices: violence. Certainly I believe in the necessity of fighting the system, and in the necessity of self-defense, but I'm *not* going to employ the same tactics and methods the system uses every day. Why replace the system with the same thing?

We need a *new* system, one where people are free of the violence of the system. I may not be a pacifist, but I still hope for a day when there are no bombs, no guns – no weapons whatsoever – no war, poverty, or other injustices; no social and class hatreds; no crime and no prisons.

I reject the tools and weapons of violence.

God-talk
ON PHASE II

Then Almitra spoke, saying, We would
ask now of Death.
     And he said:
     You would know the secret of death.
     But how shall you find it unless you seek
it in the heart of life?
     The owl whose night-bound eyes are
blind unto the day cannot unveil the mystery
of light.
     If you would indeed behold the spirit of
death, open your heart wide unto the body
of life.
     For life and death are one, even as
river and the sea are one.

Kahlil Gibran, *The Prophet*

ON DEATH'S BRINK, men begin to see things they've
perhaps never seen before. Like those around them, and
especially those who share their fate. Men on Phase II –
men whose death warrants have been signed, men with
a date to die – live each day with a clarity and vibrancy
they might have lacked in less pressured times. In the
state's ice-box, behind the clear plastic shield that separates death row proper from Phase II, sounds from the
six death warrant cells are muffled from the rest of
the block.

Men on the "Faze" spend their precious hours doing whatever concerns them most, and for many that means talking and learning about each other, their depths, their heights, their human uniqueness.

It is midnight, the end of a long, humid July day, yet conversation continues in earnest:

"You ever think of outer space?"
"Hell, yeah!"
"Really?"
"Yeah, man – alla time."
"No shit? Like what kinda stuff?"
"All kindsa stuff – like the vastness of space, black holes, how impossible a lotta that stuff they show on sci-fi movies is; inner space...a lotta stuff, Scott."
"Humph. Well, tell me summa the stuff you be thinkin' of, Mu – break down what you mean."
"Well, you know how in alla star wars and star trek-type joints, when a ship gets hit, you hear these huge KA-BOOM! explosions, and see fire balls and shit?"
"Uh-huh."
"That's impossible."
"Why you say that?"
"Coz. Dig – in space, there's a vacuum – no oxygen – so how can sound travel? To the extent there'd be an explosion, it would be silent."
"OK. What other stuff?"
"Well, you know how dudes ina movie talk about light-

speed, 'warp factor seven,' and all that?"

"Uh-huh."

"Dig this, Scott. The smallest sub-atomic particle in light is the photon; that's what's movin' atta speed of light, and it moves so quickly 'coz it got no mass. Once you add mass, a ship, provisions, human bodies, you slow everything down – so all that warp seven, faster-than-light stuff is impossible."

"Damn, Mu – how'd you get into that shit?"

"I read. Science. Einstein. Stephen Hawking. Science fiction. Asimov. Herbert. Bisson – alla them dudes."

"No shit, Mu! All right. Here's one for ya: What, or who is God? Whoa! Do you believe in God?"

"Absolutely."

"Well?"

"Each man, based on his own understanding, creates his own gods. Every person in creation has his own idea of God. Now, are they all wrong? Yes – and no.

"Everybody worships somethin'. They might not give it the name 'God,' but what they spend their time, their minds, their consciousness on – that's their God. It might be money; drugs; sex. The communists in Russia wouldn't say it in those words, but Marx and Lenin were gods to them, even though they claimed to re-nounce religion.

"God is divine intelligence. God is life. God is the force that keeps this creation in existence."

"But *who* is God? What's his name?"

"Why *his?*"

"What you mean, man?"

"I mean – dig this…There's hundreds of names for God, right?"

"Yup – "

"Man gave God these names, based on culture, history, their own perceptions – so, how dya think 'God' got sex – a God that created both sexes?"

"You sayin' God's a female?"

"Naw, man – I ain't saying God is a woman; I'm saying God is beyond man or woman – beyond sex, and therefore as much mother, if not more so, as father."

"How can you say that, man? You just said 'beyond woman.' How can God be beyond woman, and also mother?"

"Well – I mean, in terms of function. Dig this. In all cultures, among almost all of nature, the mother is she who truly cares, who feeds, cleans, hugs – y' know? – for all her children. Think of mother earth: all that we know, that we see, that we eat, that we wear, comes from mother earth. Man might combine things, mix things up, but he don't create nothin.' Mama – God – creates or brings into creation all that is. Think of it this way, Scott…"

"I'm wicha, Mu…"

"Of all the planets in this entire solar system: why is Earth just right for us? Mars and Venus? Too hot. Jupiter? Too gaseous. Pluto? Too cold. This Earth is *just* right! That ain't no coincidence, man."

"Hey, man. I was just checkin' you out. I've often
thought those exact, same things – I didn't know *you*
wuz into that, man – I had no idea!"

"Why not?"

"Well, I knew you was into nature – but this stuff?"

"Hey – ain't God 'natural'? Ain't Earth? Ain't all of
creation – all that is?"

"I know that, man – but – hey! I'm surprised!"

"Well, to be perfectly honest, I'm surprised too!"

"Yeah? Now don't go off on me, but…"

"I ain't – why?"

"Well, I thought you wuza bona-fide *nut!*" Scott erupts
ina fit of laughter –

"I'm serious, man."

His laughter continues…

"See, down Huntington, guys said you wuza secret
squirrel-type dude – talkin 'bout spies 'n' shit, real crazy
stuff…When you told me 'bout gov'ment files, I looked
to my own experience. Y'know, the gov'ment bugged
me for years and years, when I was in my young
teens – "

"Oh yeah?"

"Yup – If I told dudes about it, they'd be whisperin' the
same stuff 'bout me – 'that nigga's crazy; he into some
secret squirrel-type shit…' Y'know the rap."

"Yeah, I do."

"Coz they don't know – unless they hadda experience."

"That's it! Now, let's get into black holes – you into
that?"

"Well, I read some stuff 'bout it – "

"Do you think a human could survive in it?"

"Nope."

"Why not?"

"Well…"

The men talk on – hour after hour, late into the night,
early into morn. Days, hours away from a date with
death, they finally see each other.

They see the miracles of life, the miracle of each other.

Lawd, Lawd, I look at you and see
   a man on a cross who don't look like me.
I wonder if you can truly be
   God of all eternity –
   maker of earth, the wind, the sea,
   maker, even, of lil' old black me?

Meditations on the Cross

Lawd, Lawd, I look at the cross and pray by Rufus, a slave
Can you hear the words I say?
Can you see the things I do?
Things done by folks
   who look like you?
Can you snap these chains offa my feet?
Can you make it so's I don't get beat?
Can you bring my wife,
   son, daughter back to me?
Can you bring an end to slavery?
Lawd, O Lawd – can you truly make us free?

Come to think of it, why am I
   asking you?
What I mean to say is –
   what can you do?
Your hands is nailed to this here cross –
How could you ever be the Big Boss?

Also nailed is your two feets –
   you cain't even walk the streets!
And on your head, that crown
   of thorns,
Will it stop new ideas
   from being born?

Lawd, I don't mean to sound too smart,
   it's just that these things be in my heart;
The last time I thought of you,
   was when they lynched my daddy, Lou –
They tied his hands and bound his feet,
   lashed him, slashed him like a piece of meat,
   cut him, burned him, and just before they let him die,
   they hung him from a tree, swingin' high.
How could your people do this, Lawd?
How could you give them the Power of the sword?
How could you let 'em hang Daddy on a tree,
   when that's the very same thing they did to thee?
How could you let 'em bring us here as slaves
   over roiling miles of ocean waves?
How could you do this, Jesus,
Weren't you king of the Jews –
Weren't they themselves broken and beaten,
   battered and abused?

Lawd, O Lawd, I ain't tryin' to be
    no big man,
I'm just tryin' to understand.
And if you don't wanna speak to me,
    can't you at least let me see?
Ol' preacher say you died for the poor;
Does that mean we won't be poor no more?
I'm not try'na run things in heaven above,
I just wan' freedom, my family, Love.
They say it's compassion
    your life demonstrated,
but I wonder, if that's so,
    why am I hated?

Well, Lawd, I guess I gotta go,
It's just that I'd like to be more in the know.
Just think of this as my personal letter,
    asking how things could be made better –
Finally, Lawd, lemme say I Love You,
    'cause you went through the same
    hell as we still do.

Holiday Thoughts

IN EACH YEAR'S wintry season comes the great festival in the West alleged to celebrate the birth of Jesus of Nazareth some two thousand years ago. To many, however, it is a time of utter hypocrisy. To those many millions mired in poverty, it is a time of bitter cold, a time of no respite from the hours spent huddled in windswept alleys. It is, they say, "the season to be jolly," but for far too many it is a season of need, an hour of aching loneliness.

The faceless millions sing of cheer and charity, but I, who sit among the hopeless and the living dead, among those who populate your prisons and dungeons of death, see neither cheer nor charity, but rather falseness, gaudiness, and empty flash. The only things not empty are the tills of the merchants, because for most, Christmas is celebrated not in remembrance of the Christ, but to fill the coffers. Who remembers that the carols are sung in praise of a prisoner, indeed, a death row prisoner destined to face crucifixion? What mean cheer and charity to those who face more modern methods of execution?

THE   WISDOM   OF

John Africa

> …You judges are confusing God's right of self-de-
> fense with *your* way of legal destruction because you
> are confused about the meaning of right, the pur-
> pose of defense, the existence of true freedom, the
> law of God. A person's defense is a God-given power
> that must not be tampered with; this is *God's* law…
>
> John Africa, *The Judges' Letter*

UNTRAINED, UNTAUGHT, AND UNTAMED, John
Africa attracted a wide range of people to a small room
in West Philadelphia; men and women who had one
thing in common: need. Their needs were as various as
were their personalities. Some sought a respite from the
social storms that raged across America in the late sixties; some, answers to the Great Questions that plagued
their minds; others sought the healing of denatured,
weakened bodies; still others the security of a family to
replace their shattered birth-families. In a sense, all of
them sought that most illusive of quarries – Truth.

All found their various needs addressed, answered, and
met in one way or another by this most remarkable of
men. For John Africa was a man blessed with shimmering wisdom, enormous patience, and powerful passions.

He did what healers do: he healed. He did what teachers do: he taught. He did what carpenters do: he built. Using neither nails nor lumber, he constructed from the fabric of the heart a tightly knit, cohesive body of brothers and sisters called MOVE.[1]

Bold beyond belief, and so fearless they seemed reckless, these men and women burned with the zeal of a new, rebellious faith, and spread the revolutionary teaching of John Africa far and wide. Living as they did in a land of un-freedom – in a city whose past may well be marked by a legacy of free thought, but whose present stands on the legs of repression – it was only natural that they were labeled public enemies even as they fought for freedom. It was predictable that their path should take them into the eye of the storm.

Yet nothing could stop them as they confronted and battled the forces of the State: not broken bones, not police bullets, not jail cells, not government bombs. Not even death – witness the urban holocaust of May 13, 1985, when Philadelphia police and federal government agents massacred eleven MOVE men, women, and children. Despite this premeditated mass murder, MOVE is still alive and well, still spreading its teaching – and still doing what its founder-carpenter did: building.

---

[1] Not an acronym, the name MOVE simply expresses it members' belief that life is movement; that all things exist "on a move."

Bombs have not stopped them. Nine hundred years in cages have not stopped them.[2] Repeated acts of police-sponsored terrorism have not intimidated them. After such remarkable resilience, the question must be asked, "How?" Who united this disparate group of people; what inspired these ordinary folks to feats of extraordinary commitment in the face of the most repressive government assaults in contemporary history? The answer can only be, "John Africa." Consider his words:

> ...It is past time for all poor people to release themselves from the deceptive strangulation of society, realize that society has failed you; for to attempt to ignore this system of deception *now* is to deny you the need to protest this failure *later*. The system has failed you yesterday, failed you today, and has created the conditions for failure tomorrow...

The brave and beautiful men and women of MOVE took these words and translated them into action. They knew them to contain power, wisdom, and a shattering truth.

---

[2] On August 8, 1978, after a brutal police assault on MOVE during which their home in the Powelton Village section of West Philadelphia was destroyed, nine members of the organization were arrested for allegedly killing James Ramp, a police officer. These "suspects" were in the basement of their home at the time of the shooting; Ramp, who was facing the house on the street above them, was shot from the back. Several MOVE sympathizers were arrested too but released after agreeing to renounce their ties to MOVE. Convicted and sentenced (30–100 years each) in a trial marked by blatant racial and political bias, the "MOVE 9" remain incarcerated in Pennsylvania prisons. They, and growing numbers of supporters across the country, continue to maintain their innocence.

What power governs the stars above,
Which makes them be,
Which pours the sea,
Which stirs the cup of eternity?
What can this force be – but Love?

Why fight over a name?
For who can win this deadly game?
Why battle over religion,
When we stand on the brink of perdition?

Who rolls the dice?
Who grows the rice?
Who brings us into being twice,
Made earth and water, fire and ice?

Who plants the seed of the flower of life,
Creates and carves with a living knife,
Brings oneness by joining husband and wife
'Mid human turmoil, hatred, strife?
What can this force be – but Love?

The very development of American society is creating a new kind of blindness about poverty. The poor are increasingly slipping out of the very experience and consciousness of the nation.

Michael Harrington, *The Other America*

MORE WAR FOR THE POOR

IN A MOVE THAT was as chilling as it was Malthusian, President Bill "Bubba" Clinton signed a so-called welfare "reform" (read "destruction") bill that neither Reagan nor Bush, even in their finest hours, could have succeeded in passing.

In this one act, by affixing his name to this legislative obscenity, the Man from Hope dashed the hopes of millions of the poor, all in order to protect his political ass.

In this age of triumphant capitalism, "poor" has become synonymous with "bad," which is rather ironic for a President who trumpeted his own poor Arkansan origins, though carefully re-styling them as New Age Lincolnesque.

Masked by promises of "helping the poor" and emboldened by the *Bruderbund* of fellow Republicans, the Democrats have sacrificed poor men, women, and children upon the fiery brazier of political ambition.

In Frazer's classic *The Golden Bough* (1890), the Scottish anthropologist and classicist describes an ancient sacrifice:

> When the Carthaginians were defeated and besieged by Agathocles, they ascribed their disasters to the wrath of Baal; for whereas in former times they had been wont to sacrifice to him their own children, they had latterly fallen into the habit of buying children and rearing them to be victims. So, to appease the angry god, two hundred children of the noblest families were picked out for sacrifice…They were sacrificed by being placed, one by one, on the sloping hands of the brazen image, from which they rolled into a pit of fire…(236)

Let me tell you: *that* was a nobler sacrifice than is this! For the sacrifice of those in antiquity occurred under the belief – albeit a misapprehension – that such an act would allay worse chaos from a vengeful god.

Why are the poor among us today to be sacrificed? To satisfy a mere misapprehension? To balance a national budget? Hardly. Less than two percent of the nation's budget pays for welfare, so it is not likely to bust under its weight. Then why?

In the past, whenever reports of higher employment levels surfaced, the news sent Wall Street into a panicked fall. Good news to most of us, it caused a sea of frowns on financial markets. It is these very markets, the power centers of capital, that dictate the actions of politicians, including their abolition of social safety nets such as welfare.

When millions starve, workers duly fall to silent acquiescence for fear of losing what little they have. Fear creates a cowed labor force which, when faced with givebacks, won't even whimper. High poverty signals capitalism triumphant.

Of Becoming

RECENTLY I WAS asked to send a statement for a youth conference, something that would be read at an opening gathering or something. When I thought about it, a question arose in my mind. This is the question: What is the difference between an oak tree and an acorn? I've been thinking of this as I think of you – of young people from various paths of life converging in search of what is real, what is whole, and what is worthy of your time and attention.

At first, the differences between a mighty oak and the tiny green acorn seem humongous. But upon reflection, one sees that the only real difference between them is time. You are living acorns in the forest of life, with all the potential, all the powers of the most massive oak tree that ever grew. You are, in your seeking, in the process of becoming.

In my memory, at least, youth is a most difficult time. It is a time of emotions, of tossing and turning, of grappling with questions that bore to the very heart of existence, and with the unsatisfactory answers often given in return.

But this is *your* time – your time to delve, to dig, to plow the rich, fertile earth of yourselves. There you will find every answer worth giving. You are at that place in time when you have learned one of the most powerful truths: that sometimes we older folks just don't have the answers.

I therefore urge you to dig on, until the treasure of truth is unearthed in each of you, and once gained, is brought to life. Your task is not easy, but it is necessary. For tomorrow's forests must be treed by you.

ANOTHER THING that comes to mind: you young adults should recognize that however you look at it, you will never again be as free as you are now, in this phase of life. Marriage, for example, poses obligations, and so does a career. So if you have the opportunity to study, to row in the life of the mind, use it. You are at a level of freedom you may not and probably will not experience for decades. Feed your mind, not just with information, but with knowledge that feeds your deeper, inner self. Ask questions about what you see, hear, and read – also of yourselves.

Again, this is the freedom phase of your life. Do not underestimate the worth and the wealth of this phase. Now is the time you can best move to change the world. And worlds can change, even if the change starts only in your mind, in your perception.

A Call to Action

The choice, as every choice, is yours:

to fight for freedom or be fettered,

to struggle for liberty or be satisfied with slavery,

to side with life or death.

Spread the word of life far and wide.

Talk to your friends, read, and open your eyes –

even to doorways of perception you feared

to look into yesterday.

Hold your heart open to the truth.

INTERVIEW WITH MUMIA

Allen Hougland

Pennsylvania's new "control unit" prison, the State Correctional Institution at Waynesburg (SCI Greene), hides in rural hills just fifteen miles from the West Virginia border. Its low earth-toned block walls blend into the grassy clearing where it furtively crouches, surrounded by multiple layers of green metal fences ringed with double-edged razor wire.

Once inside, video producer Thomas Filmyer and I follow a genial female administrator through the stark bright corridors, passing through a series of sliding metal security doors to a cubicle where we will spend 90 minutes with Mumia Abu-Jamal.

As we enter the little cinderblock room, the official places herself outside; the door remains open during the interview. Mumia is already seated, wearing a blue cotton shirt and steel handcuffs, long dreadlocks hanging over his shoulders. Appearing healthy and relaxed, he seems eager to begin talking. His deep voice echoes as it filters through narrow strips of screen at the ends of the thick Plexiglas barrier that separates him from us.

AH: Can you tell us who you are, in your own words?

MAJ: My name is Mumia Abu-Jamal. I'm in my early forties. I've been on death row since July of 1982 –

in fact, I've been on several death rows in Pennsylvania, in the United States of America. Despite my penal status I'm a writer, a journalist, a columnist, and a professional revolutionary.

AH: And you grew up in Philadelphia?

MAJ: I spent much of my youth in Philadelphia. As part of my membership in the Black Panther Party, I also spent time in other cities, working in other chapters of that organization. The bulk of my most formative years were spent in North Philly, in the heart of North Philadelphia.

AH: How would you describe your childhood there?

MAJ: Average – absolutely unremarkable. Except, one would have to admit, for my exposure to the Black Panther Party, there's nothing remarkable about my childhood that distinguishes me from millions of other young kids of my generation. I grew up in a poor neighborhood, in what's commonly called the "peejays" or the projects, and spent most of my educational years in Philadelphia, in elementary schools, junior high schools, and high schools. What makes it really unremarkable is the context of the times we're talking about – the late sixties and early seventies, which was the explosion era of the black liberation movement. So there were many people of my generation who were active in the Black Panther Party, the Republic of New

Africa, the Southern Nonviolent Coordinating Committee, the Nation of Islam, and other organizations that
were overtly active at that time.

AH: You were born with a different name – not Mumia
Abu-Jamal, but Wesley Cook, right?

MAJ: Yes.

AH: When and why did you change your name?

MAJ: It was a change that took place over a transition
of years – not one day it was one name, and another
day the next. Again, in the context of the times, in the
years when the black liberation movement was growing and attracting the adherence of people who believed in that movement, many of us took African
names. One of my teachers in a black high school in
Philadelphia was actually a Kenyan who had come to
teach Swahili. And it was his practice in his Swahili class
to give names to students that were African. So that
was my name: Mumia.

AH: And then the Abu-Jamal?

MAJ: Well, I'm actually named after my first son. It
means "father of Jamal," and my first son is named
Jamal. It's kind of a mix, in that my first name is
Swahili, and my middle and last names are Arabic.

AH: How did your involvement with the Panthers go,
and how did it not go, and how did it come to an end?

MAJ: I remember – and of course we're talking about decades ago now – but I remember it was probably one of the most exciting and liberational times of my life. Of course, for most people, their teen years are a time of freedom. Mine were a time of ultra, super freedom. It was a tremendous learning experience. The very fact that I, even from this place, am a journalist who writes and communicates with thousands and thousands of people every week – its embryo can be found in the fact that I worked as a Panther in what's called the Ministry of Information. That means I worked filing reports to the national Black Panther Party journal called *Black Panther – Black Community News Service* based in San Francisco and Oakland, California. But we also had regional papers that came out, like throw-aways or give-aways. I worked for the Ministry of Information in Philadelphia, in New York, and in other cities. So I was trained as a revolutionary journalist, trained to present the positions of the Black Panther Party from that revolutionary – black revolutionary – perspective.

I should add that many times, people will talk about that experience of mine, not from a position of knowledge, but from a position of opinion, and say, "well, that wasn't 'mainstream' journalism" or "when did you get into 'mainstream' journalism?" Of course, I hold that that experience *was* one of mainstream journalism. What does mainstream journalism mean if it does not mean that someone writes, edits, does graphic arts – because in the

Party we learned to do everything – for a newspaper
that is read by over 250,000 people a week? How many
papers have a circulation that expansive? It was an international circulation. We covered international news, we
made international news. Because at one point, at the
Party's highest point – before COINTELPRO ripped it
asunder – came the establishment of the Party's international office in North Africa, in Algiers. It was called the
Inter-communal Section, under the former Minister of
Information, Eldridge Cleaver. In essence, it was African-
America's first international embassy – an independent
embassy of revolutionary African-America, where people
all over the world could come and talk without the
intercession of the United States Government.

And I say "without the intercession of the United States
Government" because it is only fair, it is only honest, it
is only accurate to point out that the function of the
United States Government at that time and before and
since has been to retard, destroy, disrupt, and tear
asunder the black liberation and black nationalist movements of that period. That's proven by FBI files that
have been released after the fact. How many people
who celebrate the memory of the birthday of Dr. Martin
Luther King, Jr. know that the FBI hounded him relent-
lessly, tapped his phones and hotel rooms, worked
through snitches, with the full blessings of the United
States Government at the highest levels – I mean in the
White House? How many people know that's true of

A. Philip Randolph, the African-American labor leader who helped create the march on Washington back in the early sixties? Or Marcus Garvey? Or Malcolm X? The list can go on and on. There's also Adam Clayton Powell, who was a Congressman from Harlem. Here he was, a Congressman, and he was under complete and total surveillance by the government of which he was a member. The late J. Edgar Hoover made it very clear that the function of the FBI was to prevent the rise of a black Messiah: anyone who could unite black America into one cohesive force.

AH: Where did he say that?

MAJ: He said that in his COINTELPRO papers, in his files. That's in the FBI files. If anyone finds that what I'm saying is in the least incredible, I would invite them to read a book written by a professor of political science named Kenneth O'Reilly. The book is called *Black Americans: The FBI Files* [Carroll & Graf, 1994].

AH: And so you felt the need for black revolution?

MAJ: Absolutely.

AH: What do you mean by that exactly, when you say "black revolution?"

MAJ: The word revolution means transformation; it means change. When one considers from any objective perspective the condition of African-American people in this country – if you didn't find the need to change that condition for the better, then your interest was to keep things as they were, to preserve the status quo. If you look at the condition of African-Americans today, we're at the bottom of every social indicator – in terms of educational attainment, in terms of work income, in terms of our life expectancy, in terms of our health. Every indicator of social well-being and status. Why are we at the bottom of those lists? I would say that it isn't a reality that could be isolated in 1970. It is a reality that continues to this day. Revolution is a necessity. Change is necessary – to change a situation that is deadly to us.

AH: I have two quotes I want to read you. One of them from Frederick Douglass, saying: "Power concedes nothing without a demand." And the other, which you are quoted as having once said: "Political power grows out of the barrel of a gun." I'd like you to talk about those two statements.

MAJ: Frederick Douglass may have said that over a hundred and fifty years ago, but that truth is certainly evident today, and will be evident for as long as men live. "Power concedes nothing without a demand." To the extent that African-Americans have moved out of *de facto* segregation and slavery in this country – that didn't happen because one day America woke up and said, "I think we should give African-Americans their voting rights; we should stop discrimination against them in jobs and housing and so forth." No, it didn't happen like that. It happened because of the actions, the strategies, and the pains and the deaths, finally, of people like Dr. Martin Luther King, like Malcolm X, like Dr. Huey P. Newton – people from a wide range of philosophical and ideological positions, people who made those demands on power. Had there not been a Malcolm X, there would not have been the effectiveness of a Dr. Martin Luther King, because both of them, in their different roles, communicated to the power structure: "We'd better go this way, or this way there'll be a consequence."

To the latter quotation, which – I should say – is from Chairman Mao Zedong of the Chinese Communist Party – that was something that was used in my case, as a justification to give me the death penalty. In the case *Dawson v. Delaware*, in which the prosecutor introduced the defendant's Aryan Brotherhood membership, the U.S. Supreme Court found that violated his First Amendment right of association. Well, in the penalty phase of my trial, the prosecution introduced my membership of over a decade before, as a teenager, in the Black Panther Party. To a predominantly white jury, some of whom were relatives of police officers – come on! What about the membership of the judge in the Fraternal Order of Police? That's irrelevant? When we raised that, he said "Well, I was only a member for a few years." Well damn, I was only a member of the Black

Panther Party for a few years. There's not even the appearance of balance here.

Thomas Filmyer/WCB

I think it only fair at this point to respond to the quote as I did then, when it was raised: how did Americans (or people who call themselves Americans) – how did they acquire political power here in this country, if not through a gun? How did they prevail over the forces of the Crown, of Britain, in the so-called Revolutionary War, if not through the power and force of arms? How did they prevail over the native peoples of this country in the so-called Indian Wars, if not through force of arms? So one does not have to say this is a communist sentiment or a radical sentiment. It is a sentiment that arises from history, and is undeniable. It's very curious how people will talk about how proud they are to be an American, and ignore the very roots of what being American came from. If Americans did not fight with all the tools at their command – including guns – against the British, we'd all be speaking with a British accent and saying "God save the Queen."

AH: Mumia, about your later journalism work. Your work was guided by, you said, "the principle that we are oppressed black human beings first." As a result of the work you did in Philadelphia and in the U.S. in general in the seventies, you became known as "the voice of the voiceless," especially as regards the group MOVE. Can you talk about your later journalism work, and also tell us who MOVE is?

MAJ: Sure, that would be my honor. MOVE is a family of revolutionaries, of naturalist revolutionaries, founded in Philadelphia in the late sixties/early seventies, who oppose all that this system represents. For years in Philadelphia, there's been continual and unrelenting conflict between the MOVE organization and the city – that is, the police, the judiciary, and the political arm of the system. They have fought it bitterly. We reporters have a herd mentality. Reporters tend to do what other reporters do – it's almost like herd instinct. The "herd" in Philadelphia was describing MOVE in frankly animalistic or sub-human terms. I remember an editorial that appeared in the *Philadelphia Inquirer* that used, I think, precisely those terms: it said they were "sub-human." Wow! That was an editorial that just expressed a tone that was reflected in the coverage. Based on what I had read in the newspapers, I could not say that MOVE were my favorite people – probably the opposite was the truth.

But I found something out that was very interesting

when I began covering MOVE as part of my work as a reporter for a radio station that's now known as WWDB, WHAT at that time: I found out they were human beings. That doesn't sound like an earth-shattering revelation now, but it was then, because the complete dehumanization of them was almost total in terms of how local and regional media projected this group – as though they were literally beyond the pale. What I found were idealistic, committed, strong, unshakable men and women who had a deep spirit-level aversion to everything this system represents. To them, this system was a death system involved in a deathly war. To them, everything this system radiated was poison – from its technological waste to its destruction of the earth, to its destruction of the air and water, to its destruction of the very genetic pool of human life and animal life and all life. MOVE opposed all this bitterly and unrelentingly, without compromise.

I remember the first time I heard about MOVE – perhaps it was a television report – in the early seventies. Some of the MOVE people had gotten busted, and the gist of the television broadcast was: "These nuts, these crazy people, were protesting outside the zoo for no reason." Of course they didn't explain what MOVE's position was. Well, what you found later, when you got closer and began examining the reality, was that according to the teachings of MOVE's founder, John Africa, all life –

all life – is sacred and has worth, and should not be exploited for money and profit. MOVE people were busted because they were protesting the reality of the zoo, which they called a "prison" for animal life. Today you have groups like Earth First and so forth, across the world, who embrace many of those same positions that were once called bizarre. MOVE did it twenty years ago. What I found was a remarkable and incredible family that continues to thrive, to grow, to grow stronger, to build, and to touch bases with people. I mean, if someone told me twenty years ago that there would be MOVE support groups in London and Paris, I'd have said: "Get out of here, you're out of your mind!" Today that's a reality.

AH: Do you consider MOVE founder John Africa to be your spiritual leader?

MAJ: Yes, absolutely, without question.

AH: When you talk about faith, your faith – because you do bring up faith – what do you mean?

MAJ: Faith simply means belief. People can put all kinds of tags and clothing on it and call it whatever they want to call it. But what you believe in, what has resonance for you, in your deepest self – that's truly your faith. To some people that's money. To many, I guess, millions in America – they will talk about "In God We Trust," but guess what – they really trust money. Their faith, their real self, revolves around currency, money, wealth, status – those kinds of things. I found in the teachings of John Africa a truth that was undeniable, that was powerful, that was naked, that was raw. And it talked about this system in a way that I wish I had the guts to talk about it and I wish I had the clarity to talk about it. MOVE members talked about it uncompromisingly, and not just talked about it, but lived it every day. In America we talk about religion. If you're Christian, you talk about Sunday. That's your religion: Sunday you go to church, Monday you do your thing. And the next Sunday you go back to church, and the next Monday you do your thing again. If you're Jewish, then Saturday is your Sabbath, and you go to temple and you say your prayers. If you're Muslim, then Friday is your day *Juma'at.* And what all of these religions really suggest in these days and times is a kind of compartmentalization of faith – "this is your holy day." To MOVE, all days are holy days, because all life is holy. When you're out fighting for your brothers and sisters, you're practicing your religion. Faith means what you truly, absolutely believe. If you ask a MOVE person, "What is your religion?" he'll say "life."

AH: What would you say to the critics of MOVE and to people in the neighborhoods where they lived who have said that they were a disruption, a nuisance; that they were dirty, that they were noisy, that they were constantly proselytizing to the neighborhood and violating their neighbors' right to live in peace?

MAJ: I would say this – and assume for the sake of argument that all of those criticisms were absolutely true: How noisy is a bomb? How disruptive is the destruction of sixty-one houses by fire? How alienating is massacre and mass murder? Because that's what the city gave people who said: "These MOVE nuts are a pain in our ass."

AH: Of course we're talking about the bombing of the MOVE house on Osage Avenue in Philadelphia in 1985.

MAJ: Yes. On May 13, 1985, the city of Philadelphia literally shot tens of thousands of rounds into that house on Osage Avenue, and dropped a bomb, and let the fire burn for ten or twelve hours. And it consumed sixty-one houses, at last count. Was that disruptive of their neighborhood rights? Was that disruptive of life itself? Was that disturbing? I think that many people found themselves suckered by a political and police system that used neighborhood conflict and intensified it into urban war and almost Armageddon. I've lived in several parts of that city and in other cities. I've had neighbors who were pains in the ass – I've had people play their music, and no matter what you said, you couldn't get them to turn it down, not unless you wanted to go down there and get into a fistfight or something. In many neighborhoods, in southwest Phila-

delphia today, you can't stick your head out the door
without hearing submachine gun fire. Is that disruptive?
Is the neighborhood alarmed when some drug-addicted
punk pulls out an Uzi and shoots at a competitor? You
got crack dealing, you got prostitution – you have all
the ills of society. But you know what you don't have?
You don't have the government come down as if in a
war as they did on May 13, 1985. You don't have that.
Unless you have MOVE rebels and revolutionaries in
their homes…

AH: Mumia, about the death penalty – with which
you're well acquainted – you have said that, "where
the death penalty is concerned, law follows politics."
And we have seen a change, an evolution – if you want
to call it that – in death penalty law over the last twenty
or twenty-five years.

MAJ: It might best be called a "devolution."

AH: Yes – from the U.S. Supreme Court case *Furman v.
Georgia*, which declared the death penalty unconstitutional as it was being applied at that time, 1972;
through *Gregg v. Georgia* in 1976, which declared the
death penalty would be constitutional if "guided discre-
tion" were used in sentencing, requiring "objective
standards" to be followed. Since then there has been a
new tide of capital punishment in this country, with over
three thousand condemned now. And the current Supreme Court seems inclined to curb the rights of appeal

of the condemned. This is happening at the same time
that other industrialized nations have all backed away
from capital punishment. Can you talk about why you
think it is that this country has devoted itself so whole-
heartedly to executions at this point in time?

MAJ: I think the impetus for that reality arises from the
same source from which arises the impetus for the
unprecedented levels of incarceration of African-Americans, as compared with other sectors of the American
population. I don't think it's a coincidence that this is
happening in the United States of America. If you look
at another North American society that is very, very
similar in its history, you find a completely different
reality. The society I'm speaking of, of course, is
Canada. We share the same temporal space, the same
continent, for the most part (except for Quebec) the
same language, the same general Anglo-oriented legal
traditions. Yet there you find no capital punishment.
There you find a completely different perspective when
one talks about the penal system – the so-called correctional system. There it's almost unheard of for a man to
be sentenced to more than twenty years in prison – it
has to be a mass ax-murder type of situation. And when
you look at Canada and you examine it, and you look at
the United States and you examine it, the elements that
differ between those two societies cohere, I think,
around the issue of race, around the issue of this

country's history as a slave society, who relegated an entire people to a sub-human status.

In the infamous *Dred Scott* opinion of 1857, U.S. Chief Justice Roger Brooks Taney said: "A Negro has no rights that a white man is bound to respect." In that seminal case, the Supreme Court denied a petition of a slave for his freedom. He said: "I live in a free state, where there is no slavery, and therefore my slave status should be invalidated as a matter of law." The overwhelming majority of the United States Supreme Court, of Justice Taney's court said: "Uh-uh, you're wrong." What they said was:

> When the Constitution and the Declaration of Independence were written, Africans were perceived as three-fifths of a person. When one speaks of 'we the people,' we were certainly not speaking of you. And therefore we cannot now give you the rights and appurtenances that apply to 'we the people.' The Constitution has no relevance to you and your kind, or to your descendants should they ever become free.

That's in the words of the *Dred Scott* opinion. And that spirit continues to resonate throughout American law.

People who are sticklers would say: "Well, the Fourteenth Amendment surely overruled that case." But if you look at that case and you examine its precedent, you will find that to this day, that case has yet to be *judicially* overruled. And where humans actually come in contact with

Thomas   Filmyer/WCB

their government is not in the voting booth – I mean, that's an empty formality for many – but it's in the court-room. That's where most people literally meet their govern-ment. And it's in that courtroom where people find whether the rights they're told about truly exist, or don't exist. And for all intents and purposes, if one is poor, if one is African-American, if one lacks influence and power, then you come into that courtroom without the hope that you will walk out a free man. That is the undeni-able reality in America.

The death penalty is unique in American law, in that if you really examine the process, you'll come away with a lot of curious ideas about how it works in reality, as opposed to how it's supposed to work in theory. I'll tell you why. In capital case law, unlike any other law, from the very begin-ning, under the case *Wainright v. Witt*, a juror can be ex-cluded if he or she has any opinion against capital punishment. So therefore you have what's called a pro-prosecution jury – from the beginning – who must swear that they can give the death penalty before they hear one word of evidence. Studies have shown this jury is prone to convict, that it is pro-prosecution and anti-defendant in the extreme, compared to any other jury in American jurisprudence. That's how you begin the process.

Isn't it also odd that at this stage of the process, where you're under the threat of having not just your liberty but your life stolen by the State, you're equipped with the worst counsel the system provides – court-appointed counsel, with no financial resources. Often, while they may have good hearts, they have the least training, because capital case law is distinct from any other kind of law. In Philadelphia, if a person is charged with a capital offense, he gets a court appointed lawyer. At the time of my trial, the fee for the lawyer was only $2,500. Out of that, he was supposed to provide investigators, ballisticians, forensic experts, psychologists, whatever. He was a sole practitioner – he had no investigator, no paralegal – he had a secretary and himself. We had absolutely no resources. We had nothing. I didn't have to be a wild-eyed, raving, Black Panther or MOVE maniac to say: "Fuck, I'll represent myself." If all he could do was get a motion denied, I could do that. But the court denied me my constitutional right to represent myself. They insisted this guy take over my defense, first as backup counsel and later as lead counsel. I didn't want him as lead counsel – or backup counsel, for that matter.

AH: Do you think he really cared?

MAJ: I think that he cared at the beginning, but our relationship as client and counsel really deteriorated – when he was put in the position of backup counsel, all that went out the window. Because he testified under oath that for four or five weeks he sat on his hands. He later got up at a hearing and said: "I was ineffective." And the District Attorney said: "No, you weren't ineffective. You were a great lawyer – it was just that your client was really difficult, right?" And he said: "No, I was ineffective. I didn't do what I should have done. I should have done this, I didn't do that." And he's asked why he didn't do it and he says: "I didn't think of it" or "I forgot" or "I was too busy." Damn, isn't that ineffective? Can you say I had effective representation? And now you have the judge saying this guy was a great lawyer, that he had extensive law enforcement experience, that he had handled twenty-seven capital cases. That's a lie. Literally, my case was the first case he'd handled in private practice – he had just left a public interest law firm.

Well, as a result these lawyers prepare very little – thanks to such small resources with which to prepare. Isn't it odd that you get that kind of lawyer at that point, appointed by the court? The court decides when that lawyer gets paid, *if* that lawyer gets paid, and how much that lawyer gets paid. So you have a lawyer who's beholden to the court for his fees. You get the worst possible legal help at the beginning of the process, but months or years later, after you're under a death warrant, you might be appointed three or four high-caliber Harvard-trained lawyers from one of the biggest law firms in the state – along with paralegals, investigators, psychologists? Does it strike you as an ass-backwards system? Well, that's the system that exists. That has been the lived experience of most men on death row. Is that a fair system? Why can't a man go to trial with the best lawyer if he's faced with death, rather than wait until he's under a death warrant?

AH: Tell us about a typical day here.

MAJ: A typical day begins at 6:25 a.m. A guard enters a "pod" of twenty-four men and announces "yard." "Yard list! Yard list!" If you're up, you can sign up by shouting out your number or your name. By 6:35, the morning meal arrives – a tray is delivered to your door. By 7:05, "yard" is allowed. "Yard" is a euphemism – it actually means "cage," because men go out into the cages here, being counted. You can go one, two, three, four at a time. That "yard" or "cage" period lasts for one hour. Then one goes back into his cell, and unless you have a visitor, you don't leave that cell until 7:05 the next morning. It's twenty-three hours lock-in, one hour outside, five days a week. On weekends, it's twenty-four hours lock-in. If you don't have a visitor, if you don't go to the law library – which is two hours, once or twice a week – you're in that cell.

AH: And nothing happens?

MAJ: Nothing happens unless you make it happen. Other than that, you're in that cell.

AH: So what do you do to hold up under those conditions?

MAJ: I'm an addicted writer and reader. I try to read everything I can get my paws on. I just finished reading two books by Alice Walker – *The Temple of My Familiar,* and her most recent book. I've read Toni Morrison's *Jazz*. I've also read *Strange Justice* by Jane Mayer and Jill Abramson, on the confirmation hearings of Justice Clarence Thomas. I try to read as much as I can.

AH: How do you deal with the fact that you may be executed?

MAJ: I deal with it day to day. I mean, you can't, obviously, just dwell on that reality. You do the best you can every day to transform that reality into a new reality. Luckily, thanks to my book *Live from Death Row*, I have lawyers, very good lawyers, working on my case for the first time. So, you do your daily thing to keep well, to keep sane, to keep strong – to stay human.

AH: Do you feel that you've had an unusual share of
bad luck?

MAJ: No, I really don't.

AH: Why have you attracted this fate, if I may put it that
way?

MAJ: I think that I have a certain history, and because
of my history, I have my share of enemies – political,
governmental. How many people can brag – and I use
that term with a little humor – about having an FBI file
from the time they were fourteen? I have. Phone calls,
mail, the whole deal – I've been tracked by the FBI since
I was a child. Dogged by them for my political beliefs,
my political expressions, my political associations. If you
were to review my FBI file, of course you'd find a lot of
nonsense in it because that's what FBI files have in
them. But you'd find an attempt by the government,
when I was perhaps seventeen or eighteen years old,
to frame me for two murders in another country. What
saved me was my work record – my hourly work record
showed that I not only wasn't in that country, but that
I was at work doing what I was supposed to be doing.
They also tried to frame me when I went to college in
Vermont for a robbery of some sort. And I'm finding
this out reading these records years later.

AH: Are these publicly available records?

MAJ: Oh, yeah – through the Freedom of Information Act. You can contact my lawyers, and I'm sure they can give you summaries or even copies of some of them. We found roughly eight-hundred pages of FBI files – some blacked out, with whole pages edited out. They wrote letters to people in my name, signed them, sent them – letters that were complete lies. This is what the government *admits* to doing. And ultimately, what that record says – not what I say, but what that record testifies to – is a history of aggression. Not by me – you can't look at that record and find any evidence of any crime. But you can find lots of evidence of government crimes against one of their so-called "citizens" because of his political beliefs and associations. Because as a young man I spoke out as part of the Ministry of Information of the Black Panther Party. And I spoke about black liberation. That made me part of their target.

AH: Mumia, some would say you have the best of all possible worlds being in the United States. That you have the right to a representative jury, and you have the prohibition of the use of race as a bias in judicial proceedings. They'd say, go anywhere else in the world and you won't find it as good as you find it here.

MAJ: On some level, that's probably true. It's certainly true that that is the law as it is written. The question is, not what the law says, but what the law *does* – what the law is in application, not in just theoretical formulation. In the very real world – in the city of Philadelphia, with perhaps a 45% African-American population, many people like myself on death row have had an overwhelmingly white jury determine guilt or innocence, life or death. The U.S. Supreme Court has said countless times: "You can't do that." Well, they did that. They did it in my case, they did it in a number of people's cases. So it appears you *can* do that, because it happens every day. It happens every day because prosecutors routinely remove African-Americans from juries when they want a white jury, when it's a cross-racial case. So what it says on the books and what it actually means when one walks into the courtroom is often two different things.

In the famous case *Batson v. Kentucky* (it's relatively recent – 1986, I believe) the Supreme Court required trial judges to assess a prosecutor's reasons for striking a minority juror, in order to determine whether he intended to discriminate. For years and years and years the late Justice Thurgood Marshall had been fighting for that principle. Justices across the country and lawyers had been fighting for that principle. Well, they won it in terms of that opinion; it's published in law books and sent to and taught in law schools. But what does it mean in the courtroom? *It means next to nothing.* Because you still have a predominantly white judiciary that protects the power class, that looks at the situation and looks the other way. About fifty miles from here in the city of Pittsburgh, there's a case that's stirring a great deal of controversy, because of a Judge Manning of the Court of Common Pleas of Pittsburgh, Allegheny County. Five witnesses have testified that Justice Manning – in a non-judicial setting, but a public setting nonetheless – spoke to a woman who was a security guard at an airport thusly: "That's what happens when you give a fucking nigger a job." These are white people who claim this guy said that. I don't know if he said it or not, but you have five eyewitnesses who swore in statements that this judge of the Court of Common Pleas said it. My point is: What does that translate to when that judge is sitting in office, in his robes, and he has a defendant in front of him who looks like me, and he has to decide what his jury looks like? What does it mean if that judge becomes a Supreme Court justice? And what does it really mean, and what does it matter, what is written in the books – if what's written in the hearts and minds and souls of people is still, in the words of Justice Taney, that a black man "has no rights that a white man is bound to re-spect?"

In terms of *Batson,* the evidence in my case is just so clear, so insurmountable. In the context not so much of what happened at the trial, but what happened at last summer's Petition for Post-Conviction Relief hearings in Philadelphia, where we found out that the Common-wealth agreed that the jury numbers they presented to the Supreme Court on direct appeal were wrong. They said eight African-Americans were removed from my original jury; my lawyer on appeal said eleven were removed. Well, we found two of those persons. We couldn't find the third one, but we found two. So they had to admit, "OK, we were wrong, ten were removed." So it was ten out of fourteen. Now, my math is very poor, but I think it's at least 71% of potential African-Americans that were excluded on the basis of race. There are cases that say if you can show a 56% removal rate, you have a *prima facie Batson* claim…

AH: You have said that you "live in the fastest-growing public housing tract in America."

MAJ: I do.

AH: You've described torture, theft, terror, humiliation, degradation, brutality. Do you stand by all that?

MAJ: Absolutely. A lot of people who don't know this reality have perhaps read my book *Live from Death Row* and reacted to it with complete incredulity. The reality is that my book is a toned-down, stripped, bare-bones, objective version of the reality I'm living on death row, in the hole – of what I've seen, what I've smelt; the bodies I've seen carried out of here.

If I wrote pure stream of consciousness, no publisher would publish it, and any reader would say it's fiction.

The reality is that this is a world that is, by design, closed. Were it not for a court order and our civil action, this very interview would not have transpired. Six months ago, it would not have been allowed. As we speak, the state of California has announced a moratorium on all interviews with all prisoners throughout the penal system. There's a reason for that. It's to keep people in the dark.

AH: Mumia, thank you for talking with us today.

The prison official signals that our time is up; then a guard comes into Mumia's side of the cubicle and motions for him to follow. Mumia raises his cuffed hands in a kind of salute, his eyes fixed on us, and says in a loud, cheerful voice: "Ona move!" He then turns and goes out. As do all Pennsylvania death row inmates before and after a visit, Mumia will endure a body-cavity strip search before returning to the isolation of his cell. Meanwhile, we banter with the prison administrator as we pack up our gear and walk back through the quiet, lonely corridors. She tells us of her twelve-year-old son, and how she does not want him to ever work in prisons.

Waynesburg, PA
February 8, 1996

Mumia Abu-Jamal was born April 24, 1954, in Philadelphia. At the time of his arrest there on December 9,
1981, on charges of the murder of a police officer, he
was a leading broadcast journalist and president of the
Philadelphia chapter of the Association of Black Journal-
ists. Widely acclaimed for his award-winning work with
NPR, Mutual Black Network, National Black Network,
WUHY (now WHYY), and other stations, he was known
in the city as Philly's "voice for the voiceless."

At the age of fourteen, Jamal was beaten and arrested
for protesting at a presidential rally for George Wallace.
In the fall of 1968, he became a founding member and
lieutenant minister of information of the Philadelphia
chapter of the Black Panther Party. During the summer
of 1970, he worked for the Party newspaper in Oakland,
California, returning to Philadelphia shortly before the
city police raided all three offices of the Panther Party
there.

Throughout the following decade, Jamal's hard-hitting
criticism of the Philadelphia Police Department and the
Rizzo administration marked him as a journalist "to
watch." His unyielding rejection of Mayor Rizzo's version
of the city's 1978 siege of the MOVE organization (in the

Powelton Village neighborhood of West Philadelphia) in particular incensed the establishment, and eventually his advocacy cost him his broadcast job. In order to support his growing family, Jamal began to work night shifts as a cabdriver.

In the early morning hours of December 9, 1981, Jamal was critically shot and beaten by police and charged with the murder of officer Daniel Faulkner. Put on trial before Philadelphia's notorious "hanging judge," Albert Sabo, he was convicted and sentenced to death on July 3, 1982.

Jamal's appeal to the Pennsylvania Supreme Court was denied in March 1989, and the U.S. Supreme Court refused review of his case. In June 1995, Pennsylvania governor Tom Ridge signed Jamal's death warrant. Jamal filed a petition for post conviction relief in the Philadelphia Court of Common Pleas, alleging 22 separate violations of rights and procedures that occurred during his first trial, and seeking a reversal of his death sentence and murder conviction. Hearings were held throughout July and August 1995; during the same months large rallies were held around the world in Jamal's support. The death warrant was vacated a few days before his scheduled execution (August 17, 1995).

Although Jamal's petition was denied by Judge Sabo, new evidence of prosecutorial misconduct and of the defendant's innocence has been presented to the appeals court. His appeals process continues as of this date (November 1996).

Despite fifteen years on death row, Jamal continues to speak out. His commentaries on racism, politics, and the American judicial system have been printed in dozens of newspapers throughout the United States and Europe. He has also been published in the *Yale Law Journal* and *The Nation*.

In 1994, a series of commentaries scheduled for broadcast on NPR's "All Things Considered," which described life behind bars, caused such controversy that it was abruptly canceled, sparking intense debates about censorship and the death penalty. A year later, despite considerable pressure to stifle their publication, Addison-Wesley released them in print under the title *Live from Death Row*. The book has since been translated into French, German, Dutch, Spanish, Portuguese, and Italian; an interactive CD-Rom version is also available.

Mumia was moved to SCI Greene, Pennsylvania's super-maximum security unit in Waynesburg, in the southwestern corner of the state, in January 1995. He remains incarcerated there.

INFORMATION

**International Concerned Friends
& Family of Mumia Abu-Jamal**
P.O. Box 19709, Philadelphia, PA 19143
Tel: 215-476-8812 Fax: 215-476-7551

Partisan Defense Committee
P.O. Box 99, Canal St. Station
New York, NY 10013-0099
212-406-4252

Western PA Committee to Free Mumia Abu-Jamal
P.O. Box 8906, Pittsburgh, PA 15221
Tel / Fax: 412-734-8315

Committee to Save Mumia Abu-Jamal
163 Amsterdam Ave., Suite 115
New York, NY 10023-5001
212-580-1022

Prison Radio Project
2420 24th St., San Francisco, CA 94110
415-648-4505

**Comite de Soutien aux Prisonniers
Politiques aux Etats-Unis (C.S.P.P.)**
c/o Librairie Le Point du Jour
58 rue Gay-Lussac, 75005 Paris FRANCE
Tel. / Fax: 33 1 45 79 88 44

Free Mumia Abu-Jamal Coalition
P.O. 650, New York, NY 10009
212-330-8029

Refuse & Resist!
305 Madison Ave., Suite 1166
New York, NY 10165
212-713-5657

R E S O U R C E S

Live from Death Row by Mumia Abu-Jamal
Addison-Wesley, 1995; Avon Paperbacks, 1996

First Person: Mumia Abu-Jamal (CD-Rom) Voyager, 1995

Race for Justice by Leonard Weinglass
Common Courage Press, 1995

In Defense of Mumia (anthology)
Writers and Readers Press, 1996

Jamal Journal (newsletter), **Jamal Summit** (magazine)
First Day (the MOVE newspaper)
*Subscriptions available from Int'l Concerned Family
and Friends of Mumia Abu-Jamal*

From Death Row: This is Mumia-Abu-Jamal
26 Radio Commentaries on Audiocassette
Available from The Prison Radio Project

Publisher J. Christoph Arnold with the author of *Death Blossoms*

The Individual and World Need   Eberhard Arnold
A revolutionary essay that explores the relationship of the individual to suffering and sin on a global scale.

Salt and Light   Eberhard Arnold
Writings on the transformative power of a life lived according to Jesus' revolutionary teachings in the Sermon on the Mount.

God's Revolution   Eberhard Arnold
Radical insights on government, community, politics, the family, and societal transformation. Short excerpts arranged by topic.

The Gospel in Dostoyevsky   Edited by the Bruderhof
An introduction to the unconventional spirituality of the great Russian writer comprised of passages from masterpieces such as *The Brothers Karamazov, Crime and Punishment,* and *The Idiot.*

Hell, Healing and Resistance   Daniel Hallock
Men and women who have found healing from the
wounds of war forge past the boundaries of convenional
war stories and offer frank personal accounts about their
journeys from guilt and confusion to peace and hope.

The Violence of Love   Oscar Romero
In the words of El Salvador's radical Archbishop, we en-
counter a man of God humbly and confidently calling us
to conversion and action. Those who let his message
touch them will never see life in the same way.

Seeking Peace   J. Christoph Arnold
Seeking Peace explores many facets of humankind's age-
less search for peace. It plumbs a wealth of spiritual traditions and draws on the wisdom of some exceptional (and
some very ordinary) people who have found peace in
surprising places.

Walk in the Light and Twenty-three Tales   Leo Tolstoy
In this collection, the Russian master of short stories illu-
mines eternal truths with forceful brevity.

Action in Waiting   Christoph Blumhardt
Grasp the joy of losing yourself in service to God and
others. Blumhardt, in his quest to get to the essentials of
faith, burns away the religious trappings of modern piety
like so much chaff.

Seventy Times Seven   J. Christoph Arnold
What would our society look like – and our workplaces
and homes – if people laid aside their grudges and began to seek reconciliation? Read this collection and see.

Discipleship   J. H. Arnold
A collection of thoughts on following Christ in the daily
grind. Includes sections on love, humility, forgiveness,
leadership, community, sexuality, marriage, parenting,
illness, suffering, mission, salvation, and God.

To order a book, or to request our complete
catalog, call The Plough Publishing House:

United States
Toll free: 1-800-521-8011
Tel: 724-329-1100

United Kingdom
Free phone: 0800-269-048
Tel: +44 (0) 1580 88 33 44